This book reveals Min
the believers, restore i
ance to the lost and d, ...mistake that you're suffering
afflictions; your pain and suffering has a purpose and it's all in the
divine plan of God. Apostles, prophets, bishops, pastors, preachers, and
teachers of the Word will discover God's best-kept secret hidden in the
pages of this dynamic book. You will discover the other side of the
wilderness, the attack from your enemies, the jealousy and rejection is
greatness, an undeniable anointing, your ministry, deliverance, healing,
miracles, and a mighty breakthrough you have long awaited! Your life
and ministry will forever be changed!

—Chief Apostle Leon Wallace, JP, QC
Founder/General Overseer
Voice of Deliverance Ministries, Inc.

Rev. Reno Johnson's new release *Lord, Why?* is a masterful compilation
of revelation and insights. It will open the eyes of understanding to all
who are in the middle of a wilderness experience to the truth that this
is just the precursor to a greater anointing. This book should be read
with the understanding that you will, after this present experience is
over, come out "in the power of the Spirit."

—Rev. Dr. Herman Murray Jr., D.Th
Full Gospel Holy Temple, Dallas, Texas

Reno I. Johnson leads readers on a profound journey toward purposeful
living and victorious combat as he provides a wealth of information
regarding God's divine plan for humanity. He draws heavily from real-
life encounters to show that the enemy, feelings of loneliness, jealous
attacks, and rejection are building blocks to greatness. An excellent book
for transitioning out of a broken spirit into a joyful life.

—Dr. Milton C. Woods
Bethel Deliverance Tabernacle Int'l
Detroit, Michigan

In this season of economic and social unrest we can all identify with the questions posed in this book: Lord, why the wilderness, jealousy, enemies, and rejection? Reno I. Johnson has made an excellent attempt to address these issues as he has given a true testimony to the struggles faced on life's journey and has provided both spirit-filled and practical recommendations for overcoming such experiences. A great book, filled with divine wisdom and practical insights.

—**Apostle Anthony L. Willis**
Pastor, Lily of the Valley Christian Center
Oakland, California

Reno I. Johnson has written an excellent book to encourage both civic and religious leaders to excel in every aspect of life. Indeed, this is a heart-stirring account of the common warfare faced in light of our destiny toward greatness. Reno not only identifies the tools God has equipped us with to be victorious but he also illustrates how these tools will impact your life. A wealth of information for a people directed toward excellence.

—**Pastor Samuel Blakes**
New Home Ministries
Baton Rouge/New Orleans, Louisiana

Reno I. Johnson's writings illumine the reality of the vicious attacks of the enemy, loneliness, jealousy, and rejection using biblical illustrations. This book is most intriguing, and those that read it will find difficulty in putting it down. The underlying message is one of hope in the midst of brokenness. It is almost impossible to avoid gleaning from the spiritual wisdom hidden inside the pages. I found myself touched by its prophetic voice and spiritually revived.

—**Stephen Owens**
Author of *The Revolutionary Leader*

LORD
WHY?

RENO I. JOHNSON

RENO I. JOHNSON

FRESH TOUCH PUBLISHING

Fresh Touch Publishing
www.arjm.org
P. O. Box 162392
Altamonte Springs Fl. 32716

Unless otherwise indicated, Scripture quotations taken from the King James Version (KJV) – *public domain.*

Printed in the United States of America.

ISBN-13: 978-1-7350-6360-7

CONTENTS

ACKNOWLEDGMENTS

The material and resources used to complete this book were derived through the generosity of many church leaders, civil and social activists, colleagues, families, and friends. These men and women have impacted my life in ways that they cannot imagine. The contributors are too many to mention, but among this cluster of awesome people is a small group I especially want to acknowledge:

My Total Life Church and Divine Encounter Ministries International family that has stood with me throughout the years. Words are inadequate to express my appreciation for them and their untiring and insurmountable contributions to my life. Also to the many supporters, thank you so much for your awesome support.

My deepest thanks go to my wife, Shandaly, and to my wonderful children. I would never have accomplished this book without their love and support.

To God be the ultimate glory, Amen!

—**Dr. Reno Ivan Johnson**
Fresh Touch Publication

FOREWORD

There are certain human-interest subjects that are so sensitive that we would rather not discuss them because they expose the innermost thoughts of the human heart. Subjects like hatred, malice, deceit, and prejudice... One of the critical ones is jealousy. This human emotion of jealousy has been the source of tragic events in marriage, interpersonal personal relationships, homes, the workplace, community, and national life throughout history. Jealousy has been the cause of the loss of vision, discouragement, fear, depression, corruption, deception, manipulation, and many such negative behaviors. Jealousy has also been the reason for many experiencing the spirit of rejection and isolation.

Reno Johnson, in this work, addresses these important subjects and provides sound principles and advice on how to overcome these spirit killers and position one's self to protect your spirit from their contaminations.

This work is encouraging, inspiring, and motivational with strong biblical precepts integrated throughout that create a practical application of spiritual truth that will set your spirit free. Reno leaps over complicated theological hurdles and serves up simplified, yet profound antidotes that are people friendly and life changing.

I challenge you to travel on the journey of these pages and be enlightened, encouraged, inspired, and educated as you receive answers to the age-old question: Lord, why?

—**Dr. Myles Munroe**
BFM International
ITWLA
Nassau Bahamas

INTRODUCTION

The wilderness experience, jealousy attacks, cunning enemies, and moments of rejection are common occurrences shared by many people. Many refer to them using terminologies of emotions, such as, loneliness, abandonment, discouragement, forsaken, and so forth. In most cases these strong feelings fertilize doubt in the promises of God and lead Christians to ask "Lord, why the wilderness? Lord, why the jealousy? Lord, why the enemies? Lord, why the rejection?"

At one point or the other, I have asked these same questions just to hear the Spirit of God whisper, "Son, this is all in God's plan, and it will work out for your good." I did not understand the "good" that such trials could yield then, but I sure know now why I experienced the wilderness, jealousy, enemies, and rejection! This book, as the title suggests, seeks to make the reader aware of the obstacles encountered in the wilderness, provide strategies for surviving jealousy, recommend tools to defeat the enemies, and give comfort to the rejected.

So often the vicissitudes of life lead us to ask the why questions: Lord, why the wilderness? Lord, why the enemies? Lord, why the jealousy? Or, Lord, why the rejection? The chilly hands of death, a lovers' quarrel, abuse, sickness, financial bondage, broken family ties, unfair competitors, character assassination, church politics, and so forth, can easily generate such questions. Yes, at times life's journey seems to take us through some rough, uncultivated, and unforeseen paths. It is during these times that many Christians go through a type of "wilderness experience" characterized by ambushed dreams, disgruntle loved ones, wolves in sheep's clothing ready to attack, and vicious death traps laid out by jealous predators. Oh, my Lord, why? Yet as dangerous and harmful as the wilderness appears, God often leads His beloved, His chosen people, and the apples of His eye into the wilderness. Why, you might continue to ask. The answer is summed up in God's desire to bring us to a place of perfection and total dependence upon Him.

The wilderness, enemies, jealousy, and rejection are all in the obstacle course whose end results are maximized abilities, utilized gifts and talents, and unconditional love. John 3:16 states, "For God so loved the world, that he gave his only begotten Son, that whosoever believeth in him should not perish, but have everlasting life." In order to express eternal life and ultimate love, God sent Jesus Christ to endure the cross with death and suffering. Who could ever forget His excruciating cry: "Eloi, Eloi, lama sabachthani?" It pierces my heart every time I visit Golgotha through the pages of the Bible. Jesus, during His final "wilderness experience," cries in Hebrew, "My God, my God, why have you forsaken me?" (Matt. 27:46, NIV). Although innocent, His fate was to die the death of a criminal—an accursed, despised, and shameful death. O the agony of the cross! The scars of rejection seem to have enlarged as Jesus' enemies and jealous opponents thrust Him further into the wilderness. Yet, as Jesus cried, "It is finished" (John 19:30), He paid the price in full for the sins of the world.

Like Jesus, many Christians often find themselves in a "wilderness," wrestling with the monsters of loneliness, jealousy, envy, and rejection. In the natural the wilderness is a dangerous place, with inconsistent weather patterns and little or no food or water. Webster's Dictionary defines a wilderness as "an uncultivated region."[1] The American Heritage Dictionary expands on Webster's definition, thus defining wilderness as "an unsettled, uncultivated region left in its natural condition; an extensive area such as a desert or ocean that is barren or empty, or wasted piece of land set aside to grow wild."[2] Indeed, the wilderness is generally viewed as a dry, solitary, companionless, isolated place. As you read this book, maybe it is connecting with your spirit because you are now experiencing these things. Rest assured that Jesus, the Great

Shepherd, has overcome the wilderness many times and He will lead you unto green pastures.

Where are you on life's journey? If you are in a place where nothing makes sense any longer, you are suffering from lack, or you are feeling secluded, take heart, God is going to bring you out. God is doing something so unique. He has set aside a special group of people who are being purified with fire so that at the appointed time, they will come forth as pure gold. The fires of loneliness, abandonment, envy, jealousy, and

> *The wilderness, enemies, jealousy, and rejection are all in the obstacle course whose end results are maximized abilities, utilized gifts and talents, and unconditional love.*

rejection bring about much discomfort, but these are necessary to aid in the removal of the impurities in our lives. It may seem unfair, and you might be tempted to ask Lord, why? God has a divine purpose for our suffering. It is designed to lead, guide, and strengthen us for our path ahead.

Job sums it up beautifully as he exclaims "But he [God] knoweth the way that I take: when he hath tried me, I shall come forth as gold." (Job 23:10). Job was on a journey filled with great, great sorrow, yet he testifies that when we are sufficiently tried, we will come out of the furnace as pure gold. This journey through the wilderness, attacks from the enemy, jealousy, and rejection are temporary trials, which will yield dynamic results.

Chapter 1

LORD, WHY THE WILDERNESS?

The Wilderness Is a Lonely Place

Shh! Be still! Listen to what the Spirit is saying. God wants you to know that in the midst of your wilderness experience, there is still hope. The more intense the fight, the greater the anointing will be. The more vulnerable you become, the more dependent you are upon God. This season of trials and tribulation is for a purpose, and it will work for your good. Refuse to give up! Press your way through because God is looking for some folks with stamina, endurance, and patience.

It may appear that you are alone. Do not buy into that lie. You are never alone; God is right there with you. By now, you might be sucking your teeth and shouting that, "this author just does not understand what I am going through." In some ways you are right, and it is not my intention to belittle your situation. My goal is to show you beauty in the wilderness and to help you survive. You are not alone. Many people, even church leaders, frequently find themselves in the wilderness. As Carl Jung puts it, "Instead of being at the mercy of wild beasts, earthquakes, landslides and inundations, modern man is battered by the elemental forces of his own psyche."[1] Hence, the phrase "wilderness experience" is ideal to describe the human condition called loneliness.

An invitation to meet the senior pastor of a very renowned church for lunch excited me. I was ready for a deep discussion. Pastor John, however, dominated the conversation. He talked on and on, and much to my surprise, there was no mention of Pope John Paul's visit to America or contributions made by Alexander the Great or Dietrich Bonhoeffer. Pastor John spoke endlessly about his church's anniversary celebrations. He boasted of phenomenal revival services, concerts, banqueting, international guest artists, and preachers. It appeared that financially, spiritually, and physically, his church was at an all-time high.

Then, with tears streaming along his cheeks, Pastor John said, "You know I feel like God has forsaken me." He continued with bowed head, "The creditors are knocking on my door, my parishioners scandalize my name, my eldest son is on drugs, and my wife speaks of divorce. Why, Lord, why the wilderness?"

> *The price of discipleship is costly.*

Many persons facing continuous struggles often share Pastor John's sentiments. Great sorrow and distress seem to shake the very foundation of our faith. At times it becomes difficult to maintain our spiritual composure, to work or pray. Overwhelmed with the cares of the world, we spend long hours in tears, self-pity, and bewilderment. If it were our enemies, we would not hurt as much when forsaken; but often those whom we love cause us the most grief. Matthew 10:36 is very clear that these things will take place. It states, "And a man's foes shall be they of his own household." The price of discipleship is costly. You might find yourself walking alone. An old cliché that stayed with me throughout my teen years says, "Teeth and tongue do fall out." This abridged warning served as a reminder that regardless of how people celebrate with you and promise to be with you in trouble, they can be the first ones to desert you.

To be abandoned and mistreated by those whom you have shared your meals with, opened your homes to, and made unnumbered sacrifices for, can be devastating. Some folks have not recovered from such painful experiences. Some have given up on Christianity in particular, and even life in general. Lord, why the wilderness?

Just maybe God intended the wilderness experience to reveal to you who your true friends are. Whenever you find someone who is willing to walk with you when you are going through your storms, you know this is a true friend. Some folks befriend us when things are going well; but as soon as the hard times come, they are nowhere to be found. At times they seem like Herod and Pilate who at the Crucifixion became friends. Our "so called" friends often connect with our enemies and plot to annihilate us. Those who never before called each other are now calling. They are driving, hanging out, eating together—all in an effort to strengthen their attacks against you. We must brace ourselves for such occurrences, knowing that "If God be for us, who can be against us?" (Rom. 8:31).

Physical or financial growth does not define God's plan for our lives. God always has something greater in mind for His chosen people. It is tempting to dismiss Pastor John's personal situation in light of his physical accomplishments. He was head of a thriving organization, and his productivity level was praiseworthy. Yet, Pastor John, like many people, could not wholeheartedly rejoice at his accom-

> *Physical or financial growth does not define God's plan for our lives*

plishments because of the personal pain and frustration that shaped his life. Have you ever felt as if you had reached the peak of the success ladder, but you were unable to enjoy this prestigious post because of some unrelated problem? Maybe you are an entrepreneur, educator, or banker, and business is really booming, but you dread going home because there are continuous arguments with your spouse or children. On the other hand, perhaps you are pastoring a church, much like Pastor John, and at church you are the hero, but at home you feel like the Lone Ranger. This lonesome road is one that we will all have to travel on our way to greatness. Nevertheless, God accompanies us on this journey, firmly establishing our pathway so that we will operate in the divine plan.

A Temporary Abode

Often the journey through the wilderness is prolonged because we refuse to keep God's command. A good example of this is the children of Israel who were left to wander through the wilderness for forty years on a course that normally took four days. It is so important that during these times of great struggle, we give praise to God and avoid complaining so that our journey through the wilderness is not extended. The more we grumble, the longer it will take to get the promise.

Some folks presumptuously refer to God as though He is a robot. They believe that at the press of a button—prayer, that God is supposed to grant them their request; and if God delays, then they throw a pity party, screaming, "God doesn't really care." God is not moved by our selfishness. God is looking for humble people who will patiently wait upon the Lord to renew their strength (Isa. 40:31). Stop complaining, keep God's commandments, and you will eat the fat of the land (Gen. 45:18). The prophet Isaiah sums up our response to the wilderness very well in the following scripture.

The Future Glory of Zion

"Sing, O barren woman,
  you who never bore a child;
burst into song, shout for joy,
  you who were never in labor;
because more are the children of the desolate woman
  than of her who has a husband,"
says the LORD.

"Enlarge the place of your tent,
  stretch your tent curtains wide,
  do not hold back;
lengthen your cords,
  strengthen your stakes.

For you will spread out to the right and to the left;
your descendants will dispossess nations
and settle in their desolate cities.

"Do not be afraid; you will not suffer shame.
Do not fear disgrace; you will not be humiliated.
You will forget the shame of your youth
and remember no more the reproach of your widowhood.

For your Maker is your husband—
the LORD Almighty is his name—
the Holy One of Israel is your Redeemer;
he is called the God of all the earth.

The LORD will call you back
as if you were a wife deserted and distressed in spirit—
a wife who married young,
only to be rejected," says your God.

"For a brief moment I abandoned you,
but with deep compassion I will bring you back.

In a surge of anger
I hid my face from you for a moment,
but with everlasting kindness
I will have compassion on you,"
says the LORD your Redeemer.

—ISAIAH 54:1–8, NIV

The shortcut through the wilderness requires us to take our eyes off our circumstances and focus on the great I Am, the all-sufficient God. Once we are focused, we can put on our dancing shoes, get the tambourine, clear our throats, and sing praises unto God. Yes, we can rejoice because God is with us in the wilderness. Verse 1 in Isaiah 54 puts it this way:

> "Sing, O barren woman, you who never bore a child; burst into song, shout for joy, you who were never in labor; because more are the children of the desolate woman than of her who has a husband," says the LORD.

You might ask, how can I sing in a barren land? What is there to rejoice about when I am going through the fiery trials of broken relations, famine, and persecution? Where do I get the strength to shout

> *The shortcut through the wilderness requires us to take our eyes off our circumstances and focus on the great I Am, the all-sufficient God.*

when death threatens my physical, spiritual, and emotional being? You can "burst into song" when you stop living by what you see in the natural and exercise faith in the God who has the power to turn your dry places into springs of living water. The same God who caused water to gush out of the rock, just to quench the rebellious

Israelites' thirst as they wandered in the wilderness, will do much more for us who hasten to keep His commandments.

Remember, this wilderness experience is only temporary but the glory is eternal. There are moments when the thickets and briers make us feel that God is nowhere to be found—as if the Almighty had forsaken us. And as Isaiah puts it in verse 7, just maybe, for "a brief moment," God had abandoned us. Note the key phrase is "brief moment." We must be mindful that God will not forsake His children indefinitely, but only for a short time. Moreover, the absence of God's embrace might simply indicate that we are maturing to a level where God can trust us to fend for ourselves. Nevertheless, as the apostle Paul states in 2 Corinthians 4:17, "Our light affliction, which is but for a moment, worketh for us a far more exceeding and eternal weight of glory." Yes, that loneliness, hardship, persecution, and so forth, are merely for a season. But, oh, when God shows up on the scene, the true glory will be revealed. God is saying, "Do not get discouraged, for at the end of the day, your shame, pain, and disdain will be turned to glory."

Folks might have placed a time limit on you—as they say in the Bahamas, "Your biological clock is ticking." Well, God made the clock and specializes in biology, and He will impregnate you. God is not limited to our times and seasons. However, God has appointed a time for everything under the sun. The wisest king that ever reigned declares God has made everything beautiful in His time (Eccles. 3:11). While your situation might look bleak, God, the Master, has stripped you of productivity and has placed you in that bare place. However, when you walk down the aisle, and those who once laughed see that your escort is God Himself, they will stand in awe. The present circumstances might seem very painful, but in due time, God will turn it around. In fact, God says He is picking up the pace, just for you. God is preparing you to give birth to an unusual blessing; that is why you were temporarily displaced.

The Wilderness Sparks Desperation

Too often if we cannot find the human solution, we conclude there is no solution. You may be frustrated because you were expecting God to send your brother, sister or friend to pay the electric bill and they told you, that they couldn't help you. Take the limits off of God! If He has to send someone from Germany to bring that money, He will. Moreover, if the flight from Germany is delayed, then God could even use the hen in your backyard to lay golden eggs. Surely the God we serve does not need human intervention. Remember, the God we serve is the same God who commissioned a donkey to speak to the prophet, commanded the fish to wire the funds to Peter to make tax payments to the government, and restored the sight of the blind using saliva and dirt from the ground. It is time to trust God to be that great I Am, a God who is able to do all things but fail. There is no need to worry about how or when God is going to meet your needs; just walk in faith. God is Jehovah, even in the wilderness.

The Israelites knew from experience of God's ability to sustain them in the wilderness. The writer of the book of Exodus declares that the Israelites' clothes and shoes lasted them for the duration of the forty years they wandered in the wilderness. These Jews were God's chosen people, an elect nation, and were said to be married to God. Such union meant success, wealth, and prosperity; after all, the Israelites were married to the King of kings. The Gentiles, on the other hand, were rejected, a defiled people and estranged from God. Anyone who is not a Jew can be classified as a Gentile. They had no husband and therefore lacked the resources to conceive. Have you ever been in a place where you did not qualify to be? Or maybe you dared to dream about a successful future, but folks who knew your family history told you it could never become a reality. Do not quit in desperation just to fit into human status quo because God ordained you to be the head and not the tail.

God says once you were a nobody, despised and rejected, scorned by others, but He is getting ready to sit you among the noblemen of this earth. It is so much better when God brings you out of the wilderness and exalts you among the great congregation. You see, when men promote you, it is temporary, but when God elevates you, it is permanent. You are the only one who can change God's plans of prosperity for your life: by turning your heart away from God. In chapter 54, Isaiah was writing of a period when the Jews were in Babylon captivity.

> *Do not quit in desperation just to fit into human status quo because God ordained you to be the head and not the tail.*

They began to adopt the customs of pagan nations and had forsaken the almighty God. Despite numerous warnings by God's messengers, Israel continued to rebel against God and joined in the detestable practices of other nations. In turn, God divorced Israel and found a new set of people to fulfill His purpose—the Gentiles. God instructed the Gentiles to raise a song because their barren days were over. God Himself would be their husbandman. This despised nation, referred to by some theologians as "Gentile dogs," became a people, a chosen people.

In our society, marriage is a huge achievement; it brings status to a woman. In fact, many women who are not married by their mid-twenties are frequently viewed as inferior to married folks. I assume that during the time of Isaiah's writing, to be married was also a pivotal focus, especially for women. The unmarried women and barren women referred to in this passage were both unloved by society. They had no economic power, and the absence of offspring rendered them unqualified for an inheritance. Many of these women married out of desperation, hoping to find economic stability, and they were often treated as mere property. Despite the efforts of feminist movements today, many women are still marrying for economic benefits, to fill a void of loneliness, or for the sheer need to acquire status. We, too, can understand this analogy, which explains the reconciliation of the Gentiles to God. The Jews were bent on doing evil, so God divorced them and married the Gentiles. It is important that we stay committed to the bridegroom, so there will be no more need for divorce.

Isaiah quotes God's proposal to this nation when he said, "For the LORD hath called thee as a woman forsaken and grieved in spirit, and a wife of youth, when thou wast refused, saith thy God" (Isa. 54:6). The call to ministry carries with it many great attributes. However, the actual call of God upon an individual life brings many joys as well as sorrows. In this time when competition is the driving force behind most church leadership, it is important to be certain that it is God's call and not man's agenda that you are heeding. God said to the Gentiles, "I called you like a woman forsaken: when no one wanted to help you or associate with you." God still says the same to us, "I know of your abandonment but remember it is I who called you, I've set you aside for Myself."

Too often we substitute true intimacy with God for worldly pleasures, thus creating a predicament that forces us to resort to desperate measures for survival. God requires intimacy to be our husbandman, so He allows the wilderness. The joy of a marriage, for instance, is the blessing of children. In nature, when a female desires to have offspring, she pursues a male. Medical and scientific discoveries, such as in-vitro fertilization, sperm donors, etc., make it easier to conceive without physical contact with males. Nevertheless, many females still seek the male to impregnate them. In a similar vein, the desire to re-create forces the creature, humanity, to seek after God, our creator. It is normally in the solitude of the wilderness that we gain a deeper appreciation for the love of God. To be honest, in those moments, the only companion we want is God.

Have you ever had one of those days when nothing seemed to go right? I have been there! As a result, I would crawl into my prayer closet, refusing to answer the telephone or the doorbell. If by chance someone came into my presence, I heard absolutely nothing of their conversation because my sole desire was to be alone with God so that I could release my tension.

The Wilderness Enhances Our Survival Skills

So often we misunderstand the purpose of the wilderness. It is not intended to kill us but to establish a childlike faith in God. Isaiah claims, "For a small moment have I forsaken thee; but with great mercies will I gather thee" (Isa. 54:7). This does not mean that God had left them defenseless. Years ago in school, I used to get into fights all the time. Once I wanted to teach my opponents a lesson, so I asked my uncle to accompany me after school. The plan was for him to stay in the distance because I knew my enemies would not attack me if they saw my backup. I am convinced that, like my uncle, God implies, "I am not hiding from you; I am hiding from them, because it's the only way to catch the enemy on the attack." My friends, it is more effective for God to teach us the value of blessings if He allows us to experience famine. We celebrate life when death threatens us; we appreciate wealth once alarmed by poverty. It is as if God's love and warm embrace steps into the ring of our wilderness, puts on those gloves, and says, "One for the money, two for the show, three to get ready, and, barrenness, you better go!"

Surviving the wilderness is about endurance. When things fail to go the way we anticipate, we often give up, call defeat, and crawl into a corner to die. Life is filled with misfortunes and delayed dreams. Some of the greatest people among us have had many failed attempts before producing the inventions that eventually made them famous. Thomas Alva Edison, inventor of the light bulb, had many failures, but he never gave up. In nature, we can see the importance of determination. For instance, a baby learning to walk falls many times before actually walking. Each time the baby falls, he or she gets up again until the goal of walking is mastered. The key to success is to try repeatedly. It is time to arise, come out of hiding, and start over again. So what if this is the third time you have attempted this project? Just maybe on the fourth try, you will have invested enough to make it work. Come on, you can do it! You have come too far to quit now. Stay the course and God will see you through to the end.

> *It is as if God's love and warm embrace steps into the ring of our wilderness, puts on those gloves, and says, "One for the money, two for the show, three to get ready, and, barrenness, you better go!"*

People often refuse to revive a failed project because of fear of criticism from others, even if success is guaranteed upon a second attempt. How others perceive our dry season seems to affect us more than our confidence in God. Do not let your guard down for one second because to put any trust in humans can be risky. For example, it is amazing how often those whom you expect to lead you out of the wilderness tend to drag you deeper into it. As the climate changes constantly in the wilderness, so do the attitudes of the onlookers. For instance, one day your allies will befriend you, singing your praises, and the next day—or next hour—they become your worst nightmare. We spend too much energy trying to impress persons who would not support us, regardless of what we do. In most situations I have found that all my efforts to gain human approval have distracted me from the mission and robbed me of valuable time. If you adhere to the perception of those around you, it will only prolong your wilderness experience, so keep your gaze on Jesus.

Lord, why the wilderness? The wilderness desensitizes us from man's approval and praise. The word desensitize according to Webster, means, "to be less sensitive, nonreactive, and unresponsive."[2] While sensitize is merely the opposite of desensitize, it requires less effort to become sensitized to an environment than to become desensitized. When you become desensitized, what people say or do does not matter because your focus will be on God.

In the wilderness we become desensitized to choice foods, luxurious living, family, friends, and so forth. The apostle Paul once said in 1 Timothy 6:6–8, "But godliness with contentment is great gain. For we brought nothing into this world, and it is certain we can carry nothing out. And having food and raiment let us be therewith content." The greatest discomfort comes from being stripped of the comforts of life. A little discomfort will not kill us, once we are determined to be content in good or bad times.

The Wilderness Houses Your Blessings

You might be in a dry place now, but God is going to bring you out. Although there is a negative stigma creeping into the church attached to physical barrenness, God is using this to exalt you. Both physical barrenness, a medical condition in the human body that delays or prevents conception from occurring, and spiritual barrenness, a decline of spiritual fulfillment and joy, a curse that results from sin or disobedience, make the victim feel a sense of rejection and lack of self-worth. Ironically, God allows His children to experience such infertility in the presence of the enemy who presents the misconception of this temporary displacement as a permanent condition of degeneration. Hence, like those physically barren Eastern women of yesteryear, we too undergo ridicule and disdain for something that is beyond our control. Do not be alarmed when God shuts up your womb in front of your enemies; God has a plan to spread the table of abundance, right in their face (Ps. 23:5). The Holy Spirit has sent the enemy an invitation to be a special guest at that table.

Your dry season is ending, and right in front of the enemy, God will move you to the next level in blessing, anointing, wealth, health, and so forth. Get ready to produce, to multiply, because of the anointing that is coming on your life after your wilderness experience. Eye hath not seen nor ear heard of the power that is about to be revealed in your life. Some stuff you have been working on and some visions you have seen, folks have classified as unfruitful; but remember that God is in control and when the time is right, the overflow will come.

I asked God what is happening in the body of Christ. Why these severe attacks and trials? We are going to church every time the doors are opened, yet we find ourselves in the valley of disappointment and despair. There are times when you do not feel like going to church. There are times when you cannot even pray or praise, and all you have strength to do is to groan in the Holy Spirit. This is just labor pains before you give birth to greatness. Hang in there, because God is about to flip the script!

You are wondering if you will ever rejoice again. The struggle is almost over; God is about to anoint you so that everything the devil stole from you will be returned—with interest. Be assured that when you come out of this, only God could have brought you out. The anointing that is on the way will cause everything you touch to prosper; even the dry places will become fertile at your touch.

When you begin to flow in the anointing, you are going to encounter several types of people. Doubters will refer to themselves and claim, "I tried the exact thing just the other day, and it did not work for me, so I know it sure isn't going to work for you." Never mind them; you go ahead and put your hands to the plow, for God has anoint your hands for success. Some will respond like Saul who, at the news of David's success, tried to kill him. Remember the weapons will form, but do not be alarmed; they will not prosper. Others will try to sponge off of you and claim a right to your inheritance. Where were they when you were in the wilderness, barren? Where were they during the midnight hour when you cried yourself to sleep? Where were they when you had to borrow school fees and rent? Or when the car ran out of gas, leaving you with no choice but to jump on the bus? You fought too hard and too long for the anointing, hence, you cannot carry any heavy weight—those that were not with you when you were struggling.

We ask presumptuously, "Lord, why the wilderness?" just to hear God respond, "It's for your benefit!" The great prophet Isaiah says, "Enlarge the place of thy tent, and let them stretch forth the curtains of thine habitations: spare not, lengthen thy cords, and strengthen thy stakes" (Isa. 54:2). People of God, especially those of us who have come through great tribulation, God is getting ready to open your wombs. Prepare yourself for the overflow! Yes, the time is at hand when there will be an overflow in the anointing, finances, properties, health, and more.

Lift your head high beyond the struggles, and enlarge your tent. A tent has stakes around its circumference. A cord attaches the tent to the stake, which stabilizes the tent. By firmly tugging the cord you may expand the tent. However, this enlargement of the tent often requires the stake to be removed and placed further afield and planted deeper to provide the needed stability. God commands Isaiah to pull up the stake and pull the cord taut. In other words, God admonished the people to take Him out of the box. People of God, let's strengthen the stakes. Stop looking for a two-bedroom house when God wants to give you a mansion; stop praying for an old Chevy when God wants to give you a Mercedes-Benz; stop looking for just anyone to marry you when God has someone special in store for you. Come on, let's pull up the stakes! God is about to bring you out of the wilderness overnight. The promise is closer than you think! Lord, why the wilderness? The wilderness is designed to bring out of us the abilities, qualities, and potentials that He has placed in us.

Survival Kit for the Wilderness

- Study to show yourself approved. (Get all the facts about your situation and find solutions.)

- Exercise childlike faith in God daily. (Trust God, even when it seems impossible.)

- Fear not! (Fear cripples our potential.)

- Use what is in your hand. (You have all the necessary tools.)

- Avoid worrying, it only brings on defeat. (God will supply all your needs.)

- Stay focused. (Take your eyes off of the surroundings.)

Special Prayer for Strength to Get Through the Wilderness

Taken From Isaiah 35

Dear Lord, I praise You for making my wilderness and solitary experiences blossom abundantly as roses that evolve from thorn bushes. I decree today that You are strengthening my weak hands and confirming my feeble knees. All fear is subsiding as I rest in the thought of You coming to save me. I will sing praises to Your name, for in the wilderness You promised that waters will break out and streams will flow in my desert. I am confident that I shall obtain joy and gladness, and sorrow and sighing shall flee away, in the name of Jesus Christ. Amen.

Chapter 2

LORD, WHY THE JEALOUSY?

Jealousy Defined

When I was younger, I would daydream of being famous. In these dreams I envisioned sharing the spotlight of fame with family and friends as they frantically applauded and gleefully cheered as I collected my awards. I still believe that these dreams will actually come true. Well, except maybe for the cheerleading squad! Too often most of my closest associates have preferred to throw a party when I failed rather than rejoicing at the victories. For instance, folks would show up on my doorstep with pies when the local gossipers informed them that the bank was about to foreclose on my home. However, the minute I began to renovate my home and while doing so asked these same persons for a glass of water, they suddenly developed hearing impediment or amnesia. It has been said that success is sweet. I would agree, but only if we insert a clause at the end of this statement: Success is sweet when you don't mind standing alone under an umbrella of jealousy.

The Berlitz Dictionary of American English defines jealousy as "the feelings of envy, of wanting what another person has."[1] In this same dictionary, the word envy or envious is also defined as "to want the same thing someone else has."[2] Both of these terms—jealousy and envy— denote resentful expression towards someone because of what that person has or desires for his or herself. While jealousy and envy have similar meanings, Wikipedia notes, "Jealousy differs from envy in that jealousy is about something one has and is afraid of losing, while envy refers to something one does not have and either wants to acquire or to prevent another from acquiring."[3] Nevertheless, in this chapter we will use the words envy and jealousy interchangeably to refer to the negative thoughts and feelings of insecurity, fear, and anxiety that are generated out of covetousness. Jealousy extends beyond mere emotions or relational issues, for even scientists, artists, and theologians have researched this issue.

The spirit of jealousy is not a new phenomenon nor is it a unique human trait, for historical artifacts show evidence of rivalry since the beginning of time. Biblical documentation as early as 500 BC records an incident of jealousy among even celestial beings. The writings of Ezekiel indicate that Satan, once a chief angelic being, was kicked out of heaven due to his spirit of jealousy. Satan desired the glory and honor that rightfully belonged to the Son of God—he wanted to be God (Ezek. 28:12–18). Sadly, this same spirit is still in operation on the job, in the community, in the home, and in the church; wherever people are, the struggles for power and glory exist. William Shakespeare, the English poet and playwright, warns, "O, beware, my lord, of jealousy! It is the green-eyed monster, which doth mock the meat it feeds on."[4] Why the jealousy?

Jealousy is everywhere. In most cases, we are either the recipients of jealousy and envy or the distributers of it. Jealousy can come unexpectedly from a spouse, children, friends, co-workers, pastors, or church folks and often for insignificant reasons, such as, material possessions, talents, physical appearance, and so forth. It might surprise us when it springs up. However, God is never surprised; He is omniscient or all knowing. Many biblical prophets, especially Micah, warn not to be deceived into believing our rivalry is some unknown character. We are to look within our inner circle for the opponents. Micah 7:5–6 explicitly states:

> Do not trust a neighbor; put no confidence in a friend. Even
> with her who lies in your embrace be careful of your words.
> For a son dishonors his father, a daughter rises up against
> her mother, a daughter-in-law against her mother-in-law—a
> man's enemies are the members of his own household.
>
> —MICAH 7:5–6, NIV

I truly believe Micah's prophecy is being fulfilled in this season, for
indeed it is most difficult to find trustworthy people. Husbands, for
instance, are jealous of their wives' accomplishments, and wives have
similar feelings towards their husbands. It was most shocking to hear
the wife of a prominent pastor openly compare her gifts to those of
her husband, presumptuously claiming she is a better minister than he
would ever be. Jealousy exists even among children, parents, siblings,
and friends.

Jealousy among siblings can be expected, as our introduction to the
word begins with such events. Genesis, the book of beginnings, intro-
duces the first human family as one that was broken because of jealousy. Why? It was because God affirmed Abel's offering while rejecting
the offering of Cain. From that moment on, Cain despised Abel. The
spirit of jealousy clouded Cain's morals to the extent that he resorted to
murder, taking the life of his own flesh and blood—his brother (Gen.
4:8). Micah is right; it is those closest to us who are envious of our
accomplishments.

Jealousy Is Merely an Attempt to Destroy the Promises of God

> Adam lay with his wife Eve, and she became pregnant and gave
> birth to Cain. She said, "With the help of the LORD I have
> brought forth a man." Later she gave birth to his brother Abel.
> Now Abel kept flocks, and Cain worked the soil. In the course
> of time Cain brought some of the fruits of the soil as an offering

to the LORD. But Abel brought fat portions from some of the firstborn of his flock. The LORD looked with favor on Abel and his offering, but on Cain and his offering he did not look with favor. So Cain was very angry, and his face was downcast. Then the LORD said to Cain, "Why are you angry? Why is your face downcast? If you do what is right, will you not be accepted? But if you do not do what is right, sin is crouching at your door; it desires to have you, but you must master it." Now Cain said to his brother Abel, "Let's go out to the field." And while they were in the field, Cain attacked his brother Abel and killed him. Then the LORD said to Cain, "Where is your brother Abel?" "I don't know," he replied. "Am I my brother's keeper?" The LORD said, "What have you done? Listen! Your brother's blood cries out to me from the ground....And I will put enmity between you and the woman, and between your offspring and hers; he will crush your head, and you will strike his heel."

—GENESIS 4:1–10, 3:15, NIV

In Genesis 3:15, God made Eve a promise that He would give her a seed, a son, who would bruise the head of the serpent, Satan. Eve produced what she thought was the promised seed, Abel. Because of jealousy her eldest son, Cain, killed him. I believe the enemy assumed that all of Eve's dreams died with Abel and that everyone where she was dwelling said, "Her God was unable to fulfill His promises." God promised to raise you up to do great exploits, and the enemy knows this, so he sets out to attack you before you reach your destiny. Often the attacker success-fully destroys the "trial version" of our promised seed, but there is no need to panic or lose hope. This seed dies to distract our enemy. God then produces another seed that is hidden from the enemy; but once it surfaces, the enemy stands in amazement.

> *What has died or is dying is just the dummy or detour to confuse your enemies. God always has a plan within a plan.*

19

God has a set time for you to come forth. The eldest son of Eve, the mother of the world, was a criminal on the run and her younger son was cut off in the prime of his life. Abel died, but Seth was soon on the way. God removed the garment of heaviness and the dark cloud of failure from around Eve so that what was developed on the inside would soon be exposed. God said, "I will remove this blanket of failure from around you, Eve." Therefore, He gave her another son named Seth, which means "substitute, to take the place of." He was the vehicle to the ultimate promised seed, Jesus Christ. The jealous murderer, Cain, was nowhere to be found when Seth was born. By the time your Seth—promise—comes, Cain—jealousy—will be driven away by God. After Cain killed his brother Abel in the rage of jealousy, the Lord asked him, "Where is thy brother Abel?" Cain replied, "Am I my brother's keeper?" (4:9).

It is amazing that those closest to you often attack your promise. God said to Cain in verse 10, "What hast thou done? the voice of thy brother's blood crieth unto me from the ground." The blood is the life. Eve's very own son attacked her promise and left it on the ground to bleed to death. What do you do when what seems to have been the promise of God is lying on the ground bleeding to death? The job you were depending on has laid you off; the husband or wife you loved so dearly is filing for divorce; the house you were so excited about is now in foreclosure; the business you worked so hard for has gone bankrupt; and family, friends, and church folks you depend on have let you down. Right before your eyes, everything you ever hoped for is bleeding to death. What do you do? Just hold on, because it is impossible for the promise of God to die. What has died or is dying is just the dummy or detour to confuse your enemies. God always has a plan within a plan. For Eve, Seth was God's plan.

Jealousy Always Shows Up
When Favor Is Present

You can expect to encounter jealous folks when you are God's apparatus or special instrument. A large percentage of church quibbles are derived from the behavior of envious believers towards one another. Cases are reported of pastors hating their members and vice versa. The ushers are jealous of the choir members, or the deacon resents the bishop. We are turning the house of God into a jungle of adversity. It is all about power and people trying to bring glory to themselves rather than to God. In some churches reading the announcements takes as much time as the actual sermon. Why? Because that is the announcer's time to shine. Have you noticed how the moderators often try to "out preach" the preacher when his or her assignment is simply to moderate the service? This is definitely not how God intended the body of Christ to operate. In fact, Jesus plainly forbid this sort of behavior, claiming servant-hood as the gateway to true leadership (Matt. 20:25–26).

> *Leadership is attractive, but oh, the darts that come with sitting at the top!*

Leadership is attractive, but oh, the darts that come with sitting at the top! Whenever God calls an individual for a leadership task, there are intense trials and tribulations that go with being called to that higher level. Recall the lives of most of the great people in the Bible; they underwent many struggles. For instance, David was on the run from Absalom, his beloved son (2 Sam. 15); Miriam and Aaron, Moses' brother and sister desired to overthrow him (Num. 12:1–15); and Judas, one of Jesus' disciples, betrayed him with a kiss (Matt. 26:47–50). These are only a few instances. I am sure you can cite many more that have happened to you in your lifetime. But Lord, why the jealousy? God knows just what it takes to get you and me to the dimension that He has predetermined for our lives.

The Bible declares in the book of Genesis 37:19–36 (NIV):

Joseph

"Here comes that dreamer!" they said to each other. "Come now, let's kill him and throw him into one of these cisterns and say that a ferocious animal devoured him. Then we'll see what comes of his dreams." When Reuben heard this, he tried to rescue him from their hands. "Let's not take his life," he said. "Don't shed any blood. Throw him into this cistern here in the desert, but don't lay a hand on him." Reuben said this to rescue him from them and take him back to his father. So when Joseph came to his brothers, they stripped him of his robe—the richly orna-mented robe he was wearing—and they took him and threw him into the cistern. Now the cistern was empty; there was no water in it. As they sat down to eat their meal, they looked up and saw a caravan of Ishmaelites coming from Gilead. Their camels were loaded with spices, balm and myrrh, and they were on their way to take them down to Egypt. Judah said to his brothers, "What will we gain if we kill our brother and cover up his blood? Come, let's sell him to the Ishmaelites and not lay our hands on him; after all, he is our brother, our own flesh and blood." His brothers agreed. So when the Midianite merchants came by, his brothers pulled Joseph up out of the cistern and sold him for twenty shekels of silver to the Ishmaelites, who took him to Egypt. When Reuben returned to the cistern and saw that Joseph was not there, he tore his clothes. He went back to his brothers and said, "The boy isn't there! Where can I turn now?" Then they got Joseph's robe, slaughtered a goat and dipped the robe in the blood. They took the ornamented robe back to their father and said, "We found this. Examine it to see whether it is your son's robe." He recognized it and said, "It is my son's robe! Some ferocious animal has devoured him. Joseph has surely been torn to pieces." Then Jacob tore his clothes, put on sackcloth and mourned for his son many days. All his sons and daughters came to comfort him, but he refused to be comforted. "No," he said, "in mourning will I go down to the grave to my son." So his father wept for him. Meanwhile, the Midianites sold Joseph in Egypt to Potiphar, one of Pharaoh's officials, the captain of the guard.

God expects opposition to catapult us to the next level. Joseph, a young Hebrew boy, found himself in the midst of some serious rivalry. God and his father favored him, which added many sorrows to his childhood. Jacob's second youngest son, Joseph, born to him by his beloved Rachel was envied by ten of his brothers. Joseph was only seventeen years old and was the son of his father's old age. Jacob loved him dearly and gave him a special coat of many colors. The Bible says when his brothers saw the love of their father for Joseph that they hated him and could not speak peaceably unto him (vv. 3–4).

Jealousy Is a Weapon to Empower Us

Not everyone will rejoice when you share your dreams with him or her. It was one thing for Jacob to give Joseph such a special attire, but quite another for Joseph to reveal his dreams to his brothers. It was a dream that brought out the worst emotions in the men. Joseph saw a vision of his brothers bowing to him in the form of sheaves. He also saw the sun, moon, and the eleven stars making obeisance or bowing in reverence to him (vv. 7–9). Telling the dreams to his brothers caused them to envy him the more (v. 11).

> *Like Joseph, God is using the weapons of our jealous opponents to introduce us to a new environment filled with glory, power, riches, and honor.*

Many of the problems we encounter are because we engage our competitors in conversation for which they despise us. We find ourselves giving them details about the investment we hope will come through and bragging about past success. This acts as fuel to drive them into jealousy. I remember being so excited about a project I was working on, I could not wait to show it to a minister friend. After revealing the project to him, I asked the minister to offer a prayer of blessing. This prayer was never given, and it was as if the minister was appalled at my request. Why the jealousy I wondered. Deep within, I knew that God had predestined a blessing for this project whether people rejoiced with me or not.

Like Joseph, God is using the weapons of our jealous opponents to introduce us to a new environment filled with glory, power, riches, and honor. Why the jealousy? The Lord is saying this is just to get you to your destiny. Some of us are destined for greatness, even though where we are presently seems hopeless. You may feel as if God does not know what you are going through and how difficult it is to stand under the darts of jealousy, but rest assured, God is using this to usher you into your blessings. Yes, God could have hidden Joseph's favor from his brothers, but He chose not to because He needed them as His special instruments to get Joseph out of Canaan and into Egypt. God could stop your attackers, but He has set you in the midst of them to equip you for the promise.

God not only propels us to the next level by opposition, but He also uses haters to refine our character, causing us to become more like Him. When Joseph arrived in Dothan where his brothers were, the Bible declares in Genesis 39:18–19, "And when they saw him afar off, even before he came near unto them, they conspired against him to slay him. And they said one to another, Behold, this dreamer cometh." Their plans were to destroy the dreamer physically and emotionally, hoping that this would also kill the dream. Hear this, my friends: No one or nothing outside of you can kill your God-given dream. They will try, but when God gives you a dream, He also places within you the ability to see it through. Even when your rivalry has stripped you of everything that physically represents the promise, God will still raise you up to greatness. When Joseph got close to his brothers, the first thing they did was strip him of his coat of many colors, and then throw him in a pit to die. That is pure jealousy.

Jealousy Will Not Prevail Against God's Agenda

Joseph's brothers concluded that they must get rid of him because he was getting all the favor. The initial plan was to kill Joseph, but God allowed Reuben to help keep Joseph alive (v. 21). God will always secure a way of escape from the rivals. It was as if everything necessary for Joseph's dream to be fulfilled just fell into place at the opportune time. The pit was strategically placed near to where the brothers were quarrelling, and the slave merchants arrived just in time to make the purchase. Surely, the hand of God was evident in this supposedly ill fate of Joseph. This was a narrow escape! Or was it just God's script being flipped in favor of Joseph? You see, Joseph was destined to go to Egypt for future purposes. So God provided free travel there and a little incentive for the brother's trouble, twenty pieces of silver (v. 28). Lord, why the jealousy? The jealousy you are currently encountering is to push you just where God wants you to be.

Jealous people always want to see you in a pit below them. Once Joseph, the dreamer, was in the pit, his jealous brothers had a feast. However, little did they know, it is the pit that leads us to the palace. In other words, the jealousy is designed to move you from the pit to the palace. When Joseph's brothers returned to their father with lies on the roof of their mouths, claiming some evil beasts had devoured the boy, his father grieved as if he had lost everything. They handed the blood-dipped coat to the father as evidence that the favor bestowed on Joseph had ceased (vv. 31–34). It is amazing how we fight each other for position and material goods just to discover that in the wrong hands, these items lose their value. The boys still did not get their father's favor; instead, Jacob became wrapped up in mourning for Joseph. Yes, Joseph was out of the picture, but they were still no better for it. They failed to realize that the coat did not hold the favor of Joseph; Joseph held the favor of God.

> *Divine favor is like a shadow; it will follow you wherever you go*

25

Divine favor is like a shadow; it will follow you wherever you go. Joseph gained the respect of Potiphar, an officer of Pharaoh, the captain of the guard. The only thing that he withheld from Joseph was his wife. Joseph's dream was beginning to unfold as he stood in Potiphar's house as second in command. I could imagine the joy that Joseph felt as he was set free from the shackles of slavery and given a seat among the government of that day. As Potiphar placed all that he had in Joseph's care, God caused everything that belonged to Potiphar to increase (39:2–3). Even the Egyptians had more common sense than Joseph's brothers did— instead of becoming jealous of Joseph's favor with God, they decided to enjoy it with Joseph.

However, you must beware that no matter how high up the ladder you climb, an envious person will be there to push you down. Potiphar's wife, driven by lust, demanded that Joseph have sex with her. When he refused her, she accused him of rape. Jealous people are always using lies to destroy their victims. However, the truth has a way of resurfacing regardless of how good the lie might be. Joseph respected his master and was a man of integrity, refusing to sin against Potiphar and God. Joseph fled and left his garment in her hands, once again stripped of his clothing of honor.

Do not be surprised when you try your best to live holy and yet people accuse you falsely of indulging in evil. In these kinds of situations, you just have to stand still in God. Potiphar's wife thought her accusation would result in the death of Joseph, but he was only sentenced to prison. Even in prison God gave Joseph favor. In verse 21 it tells us: "But the LORD was with Joseph, and shewed him mercy, and gave him favour in the sight of the keeper of the prison." He became the head jailor, and at the same time begun operating in his calling of interpreting dreams (v. 22). It does not matter which road God chooses to take you to your destiny; be assured you will get there. In prison were two officers of the Pharaoh, his baker and butler, who had offended the king (40:1). These two men were destined to change the course of Joseph's life and lead him into the more permanent blessing. One night each of them had a disturbing dream (v. 5). They sought interpretations from Joseph. It is amazing how the same tool can cause so much hardship, yet it can be the vehicle to our fortune; a dream in Joseph's case. The butler was restored back to his position, while the baker was hanged (vv. 21–22).

Pharaoh later had two disturbing dreams (41:1–7). He demanded that someone interpret his dreams or all the magicians would be killed. The butler remembered Joseph and told Pharaoh about him, so Joseph was called out of prison to interpret the dreams (vv. 9–14). The news of your gifting and abilities will spread when the time is right.

Joseph in Charge of Egypt

So Pharaoh asked them, "Can we find anyone like this man, one in whom is the spirit of God?" Then Pharaoh said to Joseph, "Since God has made all this known to you, there is no one so discerning and wise as you. You shall be in charge of my palace, and all my people are to submit to your orders. Only with respect to the throne will I be greater than you." So Pharaoh said to Joseph, "I hereby put you in charge of the whole land of Egypt." Then Pharaoh took his signet ring from his finger and put it on Joseph's finger. He dressed him in robes of fine linen and put a gold chain around his neck. He had him ride in a chariot as his second-in-command, and men shouted before him, "Make way!" Thus he put him in charge of the whole land of Egypt. Then Pharaoh said to Joseph, "I am Pharaoh, but without your word no one will lift hand or foot in all Egypt."

—GENESIS 41:38–44, NIV

No matter what you are going through right now, the attacks of envious, wicked, and hateful people will help take you to your destiny. Joseph was thirty years old when he stood before Pharaoh. After thirteen years, he finally understood why the jealousy. Joseph became second in command in Egypt; even the Egyptians had to answer to him. God's promise concerning you shall come to pass because God said it.

Jealousy Is an Opportunity to Love the Haters

Jealous folks are ordained to usher the recipient into a vineyard of blessing while being stripped of prosperity themselves. Once I discover weapons of jealousy forming against me, it gives me a spiritual anger and boldness that propels me to excel more and more. When we encounter people in our lives who want to define what we can and cannot do, we must show them that we are not limited to their expectations. Remember, it does not matter how the enemy comes up against you; at the end of the day, it is all about God's will. Double your efforts, increase your fight, and tap into God even more.

The more the envy, the more we must pray, fast, study, and praise. These are our tools that, when used in abundance, will defeat the terror of jealousy. That which God spoke concerning Joseph was rapidly unfolding; Joseph was now the big boss in charge. Everything that Joseph went through on his way to the palace caused him to develop character and become more

> *It does not matter which road God chooses to take you to your destiny; be assured you will get there.*

like Christ. When his brothers arrived in Egypt from the land of Canaan to buy corn, Joseph knew them, but they did not recognize him. It was the Lord's doing.

Joseph gave his brothers the corn they needed while secretly returning their monies to them. He did not become bitter because of what he went through; instead, he became better. He embraced them with love, fellowshipped over a meal, and sent them with an overflow to Canaan with the request to bring back Jacob, his father, and the rest of his kindred. Upon their return, Joseph introduced his father and entire family to Pharaoh, and he gave them the land of Goshen. In Genesis 47:12, the Bible declares, "And Joseph nourished his father, and his brethren, and all his father's household, with bread, according to their families." This same Joseph was despised, rejected, and mistreated.

When we have the edge over our adversary, we must not take vengeance. God exalts us, so we can help others, even those who are envious of our achievements. Our hearts must be pure when we have the upper hand on our foes. When Jacob, Joseph's father, died, this was really a good time for revenge; but instead Joseph promised the brothers security (50:18–21). They were afraid that Joseph would kill them or throw them into prison because, after all, this is what their previous behavior deserved. The brothers were guilty and were prepared to suffer the consequences, but Joseph rewarded them with love. It is difficult to embrace someone who has set out to destroy us, but God requires that we bless and not curse him or her. It is a better testimony when we can declare, "when my enemy was hungry, I fed him" (see Romans 12:20) as opposed to "I shut the door in his face." Joseph said to his brothers in Genesis 45:5, "Now therefore be not grieved, nor angry with yourselves, that ye sold me hither: for God did send me before you to preserve life." At the end of the day, the people that became envious of you will look and say, 'If I only knew."

Jealousy and Prestige Are Long-term Companions

Jealousy often follows prestige, promotion, and honor. A good example of this is found in the account of the book of Daniel. Daniel, like Joseph, was known for divine favor among great men and was skilled in the interpretation of dreams. Daniel, one of the major prophets, was led into exile in Babylon. Around 605 BC, King Nebuchadnezzar requested that a delegation of Hebrew men be brought into the palace to serve him. Among these were Daniel, Shadrach, Meshach, and Abednego. It so happened that Nebuchadnezzar had a vision of a large statue with a chest of silver and legs of bronze. None of the sages in the palace were able to interpret the dream.

The king in his frustration set a decree to take the lives of the men if his dream was not interpreted (Dan 2:5). Daniel, a man who feared the Lord and inquired of Him in prayer daily, was able to interpret

Nebuchadnezzar's dream and so spare the lives of those wise men. Daniel was then promoted to a position of great authority.

The Bible says our gifts will make room for us, and so it was in the case of Daniel. The king had a dream, and Daniel was able to interpret it. God will create a situation just for revelation, where those who think they do not need you will come to ask for your help. God has some folks in certain positions just to be problem solvers for those who sit in seats of authority. You just might be one of those persons. Although you may not be recognized as such yet, when the problems arise, God will pull you from the back to the front to solve them. Daniel was the only one capable of interpreting the dream. Hence, he was rewarded handsomely and given a prestigious post among the governors (v. 48).

> *Jealousy often follows prestige, promotion, and honor.*

Also it tells us in Daniel 6, how King Darius promoted Daniel above the presidents and princes because an excellent spirit was in him. This made the leaders jealous and very upset, and they sought to find a course to destroy Daniel. They could find nothing against him, but they took note that Daniel prayed three times a day, and so they decided to use his prayer life as a target. Wow, people will stoop to any level to bring us down. These men were willing to bring charges against Daniel for praying. He was found guilty and thrown to hungry lions, but these were powerless over Daniel. It seemed that when the enemy really wants to destroy us, he would attack even our very worship of God. Instead of the leaders rejoicing with Daniel, they looked for ways to destroy him. If you are looking for the support of jealous folks, you are setting yourself up for a big disappointment. We have to pat ourselves on the back and say, "I am proud of you, keep up the good work." Jealousy will cause folks to forget your kindness and despise your help.

In Daniel 2:49 it tells how Daniel's promotion resulted in the promotion of three other Hebrew men: Shadrach, Meshach, and Abednego. Daniel was not self-centered, looking out only for his own good; he wanted to see everyone in the house blessed. Before the promotion, the Hebrews were not targeted; they went back and forth without any obstacles. Nevertheless, when they received the post of honor, these men were the focus of attention and they became bait for their allies' fury.

Jealous Folks Are Attacking, but I Am Still Standing

God's blessings sometimes are received in stages. Because of that, you might have to endure several forms of hardship in order to realize the fullness of the blessing. If Daniel's friends Shadrach, Meshach, and Abednego had given in to the trickery of the Chaldeans, they would have missed the second promotion. God is a teaser at times. He gives us increments of blessings to encourage us to follow His guidance. Then, once we remain faithful in the abundance of trials, the bountiful blessings are showered upon us. The Hebrew boys were not concerned with the first blessing because they understood God was not limited by human standards. Their ultimate goal was to see what the end held for them.

Once the adversaries glimpse our success, they would begin to plot ways to annihilate us. It is almost as if you have to hide your accomplishments just to survive. There were times when I contemplated "watering down" my talents to avoid confrontation with the enemy. For example, I thought maybe if I did not whoop when I preached, then maybe the rivals would stop scandalizing my name. However, I found that every time I got the microphone in my hand, the Lord released a heavy anointing upon me that propelled me to "preach down the roof." This made matters worse because my opponents, upon seeing this, set out to find some accusations to detour people from embracing the word. Why the jealousy? Do not mind how they greet you with that big grin and flattering speech. Those jealous folks are watching your blessings. Nevertheless, they can do nothing to stop them.

When certain Chaldeans came and saw the Hebrew boys serving with excellence, they devised a plot that was supposed to terminate them. These envious men had their mind on the Hebrew boys because of their former promotion (Dan 2:49). What they did not realize was that the Hebrews' promotion was ordained by God, even though the king presented it. Therefore, no one could demote these men. I would rather have a promotion from God than any from man. When God blesses you, Solomon says it is forever; no man can add to it, and no man can take away from it (Eccles. 3:14).

You have to go through *this* in order to get to *that*—the promise. You may have to be lied about, criticized, scandalized, walked on, talked about, and go through financial struggles or vicious attacks from competitors. However, remember it is all designed to get you to a place where it will blow your enemies' minds. I'd rather weep now because when I come out, the same people laughing will have to bow down and say, "Surely God's hand is upon him."

A ninety feet high statue of the king was erected and a dedication ceremony was planned where all the leaders were expected to attend, to bow to the statue, and to worship it. This pleased the king because he considered himself a God. When people desire power and popularity more than serving God, they are bound to switch on you. The king's heart was filled with pride. However, in the midst of the king's quest for power, God had a plan to humble him. The king said to the counselors and leaders, "When you hear the music, you are to bow before the statue." (See Daniel 3:5.) The envious folks preyed on the king's emotions and deceived him into betraying Daniel's

> *You have to go through this in order to get to that—the promise.*

friends and thus set a trap for the Hebrew boys. Nonetheless, God's favor requires you to stand for holiness even when your life is at stake. No matter how your rivals oppose you, do not bow. Bowing to the gods of this world will only result in a temporary blessing. It is more lucrative to wait for the appropriate time, rather than settle for less than what God has for us.

Yes, the enemy will try to push you in a corner where you feel as if you have to bow, but if you would only hold on a little longer, your change will come. Do not be afraid when your opponents seek the cooperation of those in authority to get rid of you. God has the last say, and once He is well pleased with you, the king, prime minister, or Lucifer himself can do nothing about your blessing. The Chaldeans were so sure that once they had the approval of the king to set this device in place to trap the Hebrews, their plans would succeed. When they approached the king, they magnified the king, praising him saying, "Oh, king, live forever." Watch those flattering words, for nine out of ten times, the flatterer is up to some deceptive scheme. They said to the king, "You have made a decree saying all persons must bow down to this image, yet these Hebrews were defiant to your commands." They refused to obey the king's decree. Lord, why the jealousy? God has a decree that outweighs that of any king; it tells us that He is a present help in the time of trouble (Ps. 46:1).

The very speech of a jealous assailant will betray his or her true intentions. The Chaldeans stated, "There are certain Jews whom thou hast set over the affairs of the province of Babylon, Shadrach, Meshach, and Abednego; these men, O king, have not regarded thee: they serve not thy gods, nor worship the golden image which thou hast set up" (Dan. 3:12). Just read between the lines of this statement with me, and you will discover the heart of the Chaldeans' complaint.

Briefly, the position given to the Hebrew boys was a problem for several reasons:

1. *Territorial*—they were not from Babylon. These "strangers" should not have been entitled to such high posts.

2. *Seniority*—some of the jealous opponents had been in the palace longer than these people had, and they felt overlooked.

3. *Rank*—these people had no formal training and did not work their way up the ranks of leadership, hence they should not be in these positions.

4. *Socialization*—they were not willing to adapt the culture of the Babylonians, not even willing to eat their food, much less share in their religious rituals.

There is no need to limit yourself to manmade qualifications; what God is about to do in your life has little to do with such. Your qualification is based on your ability to withstand the daggers of envy. All along, the king was impressed with the Hebrew boys' loyalty, until those Chaldeans alluded to their disrespect of the king's decree. People are using this tactic today. Their goal is to make you out to appear rebellious to authority. Sometimes, they get close enough to your leader just to whisper in his or her ear that you are not paying allegiance to them. And unless he or she is truly in God, this is believed and you become blacklisted.

> *They were carrying around an anointing that not even fire could destroy.*

You must understand that those people who are attacking you are being used by God to get you to your promotion. Some folks do not like to go through the attacks of their haters because of the pain and stress in which it leaves them. It is amazing how initially this king had so much respect for the Hebrew boys, but in two minutes after the accusations, he was ready to kill them. How can the king go from promoting the boys to wanting to kill them? Those trials were designed to get out of the Hebrew boys what they did not even know was on the inside of them. They were carrying around an anointing that not even fire could destroy.

Jealous people often try to persuade you to believe otherwise. The king thought he could sway their decision by offering the Hebrew boys a second chance to bow; but not even a second chance could change their minds. There are people hanging around you who feel that they are so important, that once they give you this so-called "second chance," you will have to bow. The promotion came from God, but the king always felt he was in charge. So he had the audacity to tell the Hebrew boys, "if you bow now, I am going to spear your life, but if you don't bow, I am going to take you out."

God is showing those persons who feel that they have the monopoly over your life that He will take them out before He will let them destroy you. If your husband or wife believes they have to be there for you to get to the next level, God will even remove them. Whoever believes you cannot make it without them—you better bid them good-bye. The same king who commanded that the furnace be heated seven times hotter, demanded of the boys, "Is it true that the God you serve is able to save you?" Oh, yes, God still is well able to deliver us!

Increased Jealousy Will Compound the Anointing

King Nebuchadnezzar made an image of gold, ninety feet high and nine feet wide, and set it up on the plain of Dura in the province of Babylon. He then summoned the satraps, prefects, governors, advisers, treasurers, judges, magistrates and all the other provincial officials to come to the dedication of the image he had set up. So the satraps, prefects, governors, advisers, treasurers, judges, magistrates and all the other provincial officials assembled for the dedication of the image that King Nebuchadnezzar had set up, and they stood before it. Then the herald loudly proclaimed, "This is what you are commanded to do, O peoples, nations and men of every language: As soon as you hear the sound of the horn, flute, zither, lyre, harp, pipes and all kinds of music, you must fall down and worship the image of gold that King Nebuchadnezzar has set up. Whoever does not fall down and worship will immediately be thrown into a blazing furnace." Therefore, as soon as they heard the sound of the horn, flute, zither, lyre, harp and all kinds of music, all the peoples, nations and men of every language fell down and worshiped the image of gold that King Nebuchadnezzar had set up. At this time some astrologers came forward and denounced the

Jews. They said to King Nebuchadnezzar, "O king, live forever! You have issued a decree, O king, that everyone who hears the sound of the horn, flute, zither, lyre, harp, pipes and all kinds of music must fall down and worship the image of gold, and that whoever does not fall down and worship will be thrown into a blazing furnace. But there are some Jews whom you have set over the affairs of the province of Babylon—Shadrach, Meshach and Abednego—who pay no attention to you, O king. They neither serve your gods nor worship the image of gold you have set up." Furious with rage, Nebuchadnezzar summoned Shadrach, Meshach and Abednego. So these men were brought before the king, and Nebuchadnezzar said to them, "Is it true, Shadrach, Meshach and Abednego, that you do not serve my gods or worship the image of gold I have set up? Now when you hear the sound of the horn, flute, zither, lyre, harp, pipes and all kinds of music, if you are ready to fall down and worship the image I made, very good. But if you do not worship it, you will be thrown immediately into a blazing furnace. Then what god will be able to rescue you from my hand?" Shadrach, Meshach and Abednego replied to the king, "O Nebuchadnezzar, we do not need to defend ourselves before you in this matter. If we are thrown into the blazing furnace, the God we serve is able to save us from it, and he will rescue us from your hand, O king. But even if he does not, we want you to know, O king, that we will not serve your gods or worship the image of gold you have set up." Then Nebuchadnezzar was furious with Shadrach, Meshach and Abednego, and his attitude toward them changed. He ordered the furnace heated seven times hotter than usual and commanded some of the strongest soldiers in his army to tie up Shadrach, Meshach and Abednego and throw them into the blazing furnace. So these men, wearing their robes, trousers, turbans and other clothes, were bound and thrown into the blazing furnace. The king's command was so urgent and the furnace so hot that the flames of the fire killed the soldiers who took up

Shadrach, Meshach and Abednego, and these three men, firmly tied, fell into the blazing furnace. Then King Nebuchadnezzar leaped to his feet in amazement and asked his advisers, "Weren't there three men that we tied up and threw into the fire?" They replied, "Certainly, O king." He said, "Look! I see four men walking around in the fire, unbound and unharmed, and the fourth looks like a son of the gods." Nebuchadnezzar then approached the opening of the blazing furnace and shouted, "Shadrach, Meshach and Abednego, servants of the Most High God, come out! Come here!" So Shadrach, Meshach and Abednego came out of the fire, and the satraps, prefects, governors and royal advisers crowded around them. They saw that the fire had not harmed their bodies, nor was a hair of their heads singed; their robes were not scorched, and there was no smell of fire on them. Then Nebuchadnezzar said, "Praise be to the God of Shadrach, Meshach and Abednego, who has sent his angel and rescued his servants! They trusted in him and defied the king's command and were willing to give up their lives rather than serve or worship any god except their own God. Therefore I decree that the people of any nation or language who say anything against the God of Shadrach, Meshach and Abednego be cut into pieces and their houses be turned into piles of rubble, for no other god can save in this way." Then the king promoted Shadrach, Meshach and Abednego in the province of Babylon.

—Daniel 3, niv

Why the jealousy? It seems as if the more you fast and pray, the more fiery darts are thrown your way. You might be wondering why there is so much chaos in your life. Trust me when I say it is just the plan of the enemy to cause you to lose focus and abort the will of God for your life. If you are on the job and everyone is fighting you, it's probably because you are about to soar on that job. If the oppositions against you are unbelievable, this may just be an indication that you have been destine for greatness. If your money is acting funny and your change acting strange, know that God will bless you with abundance. Do not try to rush it; pace yourself, and walk softly with God. Always remember that the heart of the king is in the hands of God (Prov. 21:1). One day the king will sit you on a throne, making you the head. It is just a matter of time for God to change you from this to that. Remember, the plans of God are unstoppable.

Our rivals can try everything in the world to hinder our progress, but God is the bigger boss. There is absolutely no need to waste precious time trying to plead our case before a biased judge. The quicker we realize that we could never straighten out a crooked person, the sooner we are able to claim our prize. The Hebrew boys, when questioned by the king, replied they were not careful to answer him in this matter (Dan. 3:16). Stop trying to explain your actions to your opponent. They could care less about the truth of your circumstances; as far as they are concerned, you are guilty, and you can say nothing to cause them to believe otherwise. These boys were actually saying to the king that it does not make sense to argue the case because they were not bowing. You spend too much energy trying to win the approval of others. Some folks just are not going to like you, regardless of what you do. The Bible declares, "If God be for us, who can be against us?" (Rom. 8:31)

We all can talk the talk, but are we able to walk the walk? God will allow you to be put in certain situations to see if you will bow. For instance, He will let you struggle financially to see if you will bow when millions are awaiting you. The Hebrew boys said they were not bowing, although their lives were at stake. When you have already come out of your struggles, sleepless nights, stress, and pressure, do you think God will let some "fly-by-night "come and tell Him what to do with you?

> *Our rivals can try everything in the world to hinder our progress, but God is the bigger boss.*

The devil is a liar.

King Nebuchadnezzar was the same man that promoted them, smiled with them, and loved them, yet he had a different countenance the next day. He was so angry that he got his strongest men to bind these brothers up (Dan. 3:20). He had to use his mighty men because God did not want any excuses when He delivered the boys. At the end of the day, God would show King Nebuchadnezzar he could not stop the plans of God. Your promotion is not in the hands of your boss, it is in God's hands, so never feel you have to compromise.

Those same opponents will be burnt with the fire that they are attempting to catch you ablaze with. The fire was so hot that it consumed the mighty men who were throwing them in the furnace, but it did not harm the three men of God (v. 22). The plan of God will prevail; fire, jealousy, cannot destroy it. King Nebuchadnezzar came back because deep in his heart, he did not feel as if he did the right thing. Much to his surprise, a fourth person appeared in the fire with the men (vv. 24–25). These men were so important to God that God was willing to come down and walk with them through the fire. When we are in the midst of jealous and envious people, know for sure that God is walking with us, taking us through to our promise. Sometimes you might feel alone, as if no one is with you, but God is right there in the fire with you.

The reason you have not lost your mind or been admitted to a mental institute is because God is holding your life together, and it is going to fall in line with His plan. I do not care how rough it gets, you cannot move out of position because the hand of God is upon you. God uses atrocious attackers to bring out of you what He has placed in you before the foundation of the world. And at the end of the day, the haters will confess it is the Lord's doing, and it cannot be stopped.

Those jealous folks believe they are winning because you are in a difficult season; nevertheless, they are being tricked. For when they think you are going down, God is actually elevating you. You have to fight with all your might; you have to tell yourself, "I don't care how many trials I go through, I am coming out." The trials of this life are only for a season; hold on to God's unchangeable hand, knowing that our God keeps His promises (Num. 23:19). Moreover, the Bible declares, "Eye hath not seen, nor ear heard, neither have entered into the heart of man, the things which God hath prepared for them that love him." (1 Cor.

2:9). It is not easy; sometimes you might feel like just giving up, back-sliding, and throwing in the towel, but hang in there because God is at work. I have been preaching for over twelve years, and I have never seen the righteous forsaken nor their seed begging bread (Ps. 37:25). Look up! God is getting ready to visit you. Often He does not show up until you are in a difficult situation or in the fire.

Tell those jealous folks, "Do not attempt to throw me in the fire, or else you will get burned."' Do not capitulate or be discouraged; we have to go through trials because our promotion comes out of our trails. We have to be crushed because it is our vehicle to the favor of God. A good illustration of this is that of a tea bag. The strength from the tea bag does not come until the water is boiling hot. God told me that He is boiling water for tea, and your jealous opponents are His pots to put you in so He can pour you out as a drink offering to the world. God is refining you; the trial of your faith is more precious than gold (1 Pet. 1:7). God knows and He sees the bigger picture; there is a bigger picture. There is a picture with diamonds and rubies and silver and gold. If you can hold on long enough, you will enjoy your promise.

Strategies for Fighting Jealousy

- Do not fight fire with fire. (Remember, vengeance belongs to God.)

- Refuse to quit. (Despite opposition, use your gifts for the glory of God.)

- Never let your guard down. (Few people are trustworthy.)

- Take the spotlight off of the competitors. (Minimize the attention you give them.)

- Let excellence be your motto. (Excel even more.)

- Compliment your opponents. (It is OK to take the spotlight off of you.)

Special Prayers for Endurance During Jealous Attacks

Taken From Psalm 27

Dear God, I thank You for being my light and my salvation; I praise You for being the strength of my life of whom shall I be afraid? When the wicked, even mine enemies and my foes, came upon me to eat up my flesh, they stumbled and fell. Though a host should encamp against me, my heart shall not fear: though war should rise against me, in this will I be confident.

God, there is only one thing have I desired, that will I seek after; that I may dwell in Your house all the days of my life, to behold the beauty of the LORD, and to inquire in his temple. Teach me Your way, O LORD, and lead me in a plain path, because of mine enemies. Deliver me not over unto the will of mine enemies: for false witnesses are risen up against me, and such as breathe out cruelty. I had fainted, unless I had believed to see the goodness of the LORD in the land of the living. LORD, while I am waiting on You, I will be of good courage, for I know You shall strengthen my heart. Amen.

Chapter 3

Lord, Why the Enemies?

Your Enemies' Hands Are Tied. This is Only a Test.

Many people would agree that examinations are designed to assess and display competencies. Do you recall your school days—mathematics classes to be exact? Some of the basic training comprised learning to count to 10, 20, 100, and so forth; then came addition, subtraction, and multiplication. At the end of each lesson, an exam was administered. Those persons who had studied often achieved high scores, while the unprepared frequently failed the exams. As we matured, we met up with algebra and trigonometry, which required more training. College and university-level math were even more demanding. However, the higher the level of training, the more qualified the mathematician. As it is in the natural, so it is in the spiritual. The higher the level of training—attacks from your enemies, the more qualified and skillful you become. God allows us to go through a period of training that advances as we move forward in Him. The vicious attacks from our enemies will develop in us the necessary skills we will need to carry out His assignment—training that will prepare us to thrive in any condition.

God has created the enemy to bring out the best that is inside of us. Often maximizing our potential requires us to go into some unfamiliar places and encounter some undesirable circumstances. Like a car manufacturer who tests the automobile before distribution, God tests us. Some cars are made to drive up to 160 mph. In the United States and The Bahamas, the roads are not built for such speed, so those car owners will never utilize this power. However, in Germany and Austria, roads called autobahns allow you to go as fast as the car can go. Because these roads were made as such, the cars can be pushed to their maximum potential. These roads allow the vehicle to express what is under the hood. God has created an expressway—our enemies—to express everything that is under our hoods—God's power within. God uses the demons to express angels, weakness to express strength, and your enemies to express the power He has placed in you.

It may sound ironic that a holy God would use the enemy to get the best out of us. Yet, we know that the real strength of humanity is proven in light of adversity and competition. The only way that God could compare His anointed vessels is by creating something or someone to oppose them, so that what is in His vessels can be proven to the enemy to be unstoppable, incomparable, and unshakable. God created sickness to express health, poverty to express riches, blindness to express sight, and bad times to express good times. The word express, as used here, means, "to reveal or show." God wants to show the world who you are. There is a you inside of you that the world and you has never seen. The God-orchestrated tests causes you to give birth to the greatness that's in you.

> *God has created the enemy to bring out the best that is inside of us.*

Lord, why the enemies? To push you into spiritual labor and cause you to give birth. Paul writes in Romans 8:19, "For the earnest expectation of the creature waiteth for the manifestation of the sons of God." The world is waiting for the men and women of God who are now being prepared for these Last Days. Ironically, it is going to take your enemies to bring you to the forefront.

I have discovered that the strategies of the enemy sharpen our skills and insight. It may not sound theologically correct to assert that God created the enemy, but in many respects, it appears to be so. In John 1:3, it states, "All things were made by him [God]; and without him was not anything made that was made." While it is not God's intention to destroy or endanger His beloved, certainly God allows the weapons to be formed, combating their full impact from affecting us. The writer of Colossians concedes by stating, "For by him were all things created, that are in heaven, and that are in earth, visible and invisible, whether they be thrones, or dominions, or principalities, or powers: all things were created by him, and for him" (1:16).

We can conclude that God has a plan for both good and evil. Isaiah expresses this more clearly as he claims, "Behold, I [God] have created the smith that bloweth the coals in the fire, and that bringeth forth an instrument for his work; and I have created the waster to destroy" (Isa. 54:16). The smith is a person skilled in weapon manufacturing. The smith is purposely created to keep the fire burning so that the instruments might be fine-tuned for service. Without being exposed to the fire, the weapons will be dull and ineffective. Therefore, to despise the smith or fire is to hamper the usefulness of the instrument.

The smith prepares the weapons, while the wasters uses the weapons, yet God is in full control. Hence, God is saying that He created the weapon maker, the enemy who are fighting against you, the instruments that they are using, all to purge out the impurities in your life. Lord, why the enemies? God allows your enemies to take their best shot at you for your maturation.

Your Enemies Are No Match for God. You Must Stay in the Fight.

When God has finished processing us, we will be anointed, appointed, and ranked among the chiefs in His army. Do we have any commanders in God's army reading this book? In the Navy, there is an elite group called the Navy SEALs. These warriors undergo stringent training to prepare them for battle. The first training is called BUD/S (Basic Underwater Demolition/SEAL) training. The first phase consists of two-and three-mile timed runs, physical training, one-to two-mile ocean swims with fins, and soft sand runs in boots. The first five weeks, students learned lifesaving and underwater knot-tying survival skills where their ankles <u>were tied,</u> and their hands also tied behind their backs. Each student in this position must accomplish a minimum of a 50-yard underwater swim. The students often pass out and need reviving. It is a difficult skill that has claimed the budding careers of many students. Regardless of the rigidity of this course, many candidates enroll for training. Like these SEALs, we, too, must undergo stringent training.

> *God, our instructor, is fully aware of our survival capacity.*

God, our instructor, is fully aware of our survival capacity. BUD/S drown proofing skills came because of a previous drill that caused fatalities. During that drill while in a boat on the sea, the soldiers' ankles were tied up and their hands were tied behind their backs. The boat was capsized, and innocent soldiers drowned because both their hands and feet were tied and they had no training for survival under these conditions. It was determined that this situation should never happen again, so the concept of drown proofing was created as a solution. It was folded into the existing pool training along with rescue swimming, lifesaving, and so forth.[1] This training gives the SEALs confidence and relaxation skills while under the water. The SEALs were caught off guard when their boat capsized during the drill because their commanders were not aware of what was ahead of them; therefore they were not trained and equipped for it. However, our Commander-in-Chief, the all-wise and all-knowing God, knows exactly what is ahead of us, therefore He uses our enemies to refine us, build us, and equip us, so that even under water, tremendous attacks, we will still survive. God in all of His wisdom allows His SEALs—Special Forces—to be trained likewise, in that, He allows their hands and feet to be tied while underwater— extreme pressure and vicious attacks. God uses the unaware enemy to shape, mold, and equip His Special Forces for greatness. At the end of your BUD/S you will come out with unusually strong spiritual muscles: having more power, wisdom, patience, endurance, determination, and confidence.

During prayer I asked God why trials come one after another. God's response was, "This happens when I'm training a specialist." Lord, why the enemies? You are being trained as a specialist. No matter what kind of attack is sent your way, you will not be caught off guard. There is another drill that the SEALs do: At 5:00 a.m. every morning, the SEALs swim across ice-cold water for developing persistence, endurance, and courage. My Lord, why the enemies? It is for our development.

We might not be swimming through a physical iceberg, but some looks, greetings, and comments by our enemies are just as cold. What do you do when people are cold towards you, when you know they cannot stand your guts? Are you still able to swim to your destiny, or do you just give up and drown? Whatever it takes, you must not give up. People will try to stop you and make you throw in the towel, but know for sure that God will use your attackers to propel you to the next level. This is no time to call retreat or surrender! No matter what you go through, you must endure the training, show up for the test, and apply the skills acquired in the course.

God is the examiner who silently cheers you on. Most of my teachers were very nice and always went the extra mile to explain subjects that were difficult to understand. Some of them would stay with me during the lunch break or immediately after school to expand further upon a particular subject. However, during an actual exam, they seemed to change into the meanest people in the world. Once, while sitting an end-of-term examination, I had secretly beckoned to my math teacher to explain what a right angle triangle meant. Hoping she would jog my memory by hinting to me that it was a 90-degree angle, I said as mannerly as I knew how, "Please, can you read this question for me?' The teacher glanced at me, then at the paper, and said: "You read it aloud, and I will fill in the mispronounced words." I tried again and said, "Excuse me, I meant can you tell me the answer to the question?" Again, my teacher glanced at me and then at the paper and said: "The answer is in your head, we've done this before." Returning to her seat, my teacher simply smiled as if the tension caused by this right angle triangle was insignificant.

In a test, the examiner is quiet and does not give instructions. Like my experience in this test, we often find ourselves crying out to God, convinced that our trials are the end of the world. Like the teacher, God often remains silent, smiling with confidence in our abilities because He knows we have been properly trained for battle. If only we would relax and lean on prior instructions, we will come through our test like gold refined in fire.

The enemy is going to rage war against the believers every day, but God has taught us how to defeat the enemy. While the attacks are designed to slow us down or stop us from reaching our destiny, God has given us authority over the enemy. The enemy might have knocked you down and you feel like dying, but, my friend, rise up. If you lack the power to get up, then crawl, creep, and drag along, but do not stay there and die! No one who is going through a situation that causes them to slack their ride will obtain the prize. The Bible declares in Proverbs 24:10, "If thou faint in the day of adversity, thy strength is small." The level of frustration accompanying these attacks seems to be magnified, especially if they are continuous. For instance, when it is not your money acting funny and your change strange, it is a situation at home, on the job, or in the church; the devil is always on the attack. That is why you have to continue your praise. Let me give you a little advice: take your eyes off of flesh and blood because some people are determined to block you.

Friends keep on running, jumping, and praising through whatever the enemy throws your way. Some people are hoping you will bail out, run away, or come out of the kitchen. They have tried everything in their power to frustrate the plans of God for your life. The word of God declares in the book of Isaiah 54:17, "No weapon that is formed against thee shall prosper." Too many of the saints are crawling under the rock, hiding from the enemy. God says come out and stand tall so you can see the salvation of your God. Your enemies are no match for God; they have tried to destroy you, but they can not because of God's plans for your life.

God went to hell's gate, pushed the door open, and forewarned the devil that a seed was coming—a seed with the ability to crush the devil's head. The Bible declares in Jeremiah 23:29, "Is not my word like as a fire? saith the LORD; and like a hammer that breaketh the rock in pieces?" Do you have your hammer, God's Word, nearby; let's break up some stuff. I dare you to walk in your authority—hammer out poverty, strongholds, sickness, division, and your atrocious enemies.

> *When you are under attack, do not worry; just use the weapons—spiritual Patriot missiles— and the skills you have developed.*

God also uses your enemies to push you into His armory that you may become acquainted and skillful with the spiritual weapons of your warfare. God is still in control, though your enemies may hurl their vicious arrows at you.

The U.S. Army has a missile called the Patriot missile, which is a special air defense system—an interception missile. It is a long-range, all-altitude, all-weather air defense system to counter tactical ballistic missiles, cruise missiles, and advance aircraft. The Patriot missile is equipped with a track-via-missile (TVM) guidance system. The Patriot missile has the ability to destroy the weapons of attack used by the enemy in midair. When the enemy shoots a weapon, the Patriot missile tracks it down and destroys it.[2] God is saying that when you are under attack, do not worry; just use the weapons—spiritual Patriot missiles— and the skills you have developed during the vicious attacks of your enemies and stop those attacks in midair.

Lord, why the enemies? To give you the skills you need to master the spiritual weapons that are available to you. David declared in Psalm 18:29, "For by thee I have run through a troop; and by my God have I leaped over a wall. By the time God is finished using your enemies for your development, you to will be running through troops and leaping over walls. All you have to do is pray, praise, and declare.

During the Gulf War in 1991, the Patriot missile played a vital part in protecting the soldiers. Every now and then, God allows our enemies to get close. This very second, you are wondering why God allowed your enemies to get so close to you. God allowed them to get close to see what type of skills the previous attacks have developed in you. The more skillful you become, the more He will release to you. You are probably saying right now, "Lord let them equip me to handle the promise."

The Enemy Comes to Steal, Kill, and Destroy; God Came to Give Life

A saying among the saints is, "Oh, I am so stressed out, I don't know if I can make it." My friends, stop raising your blood pressure and giving yourself stomach ulcers; God has the enemy under your feet. Take a minute, pick up your Bible, and read Matthew 6:25–34:

Do Not Worry

Therefore I tell you, do not worry about your life, what you will eat or drink; or about your body, what you will wear. Is not life more important than food, and the body more important than clothes? Look at the birds of the air; they do not sow or reap or store away in barns, and yet your heavenly Father feeds them. Are you not much more valuable than they? Who of you by worrying can add a single hour to his life? And why do you worry about clothes? See how the lilies of the field grow. They do not labor or spin. Yet I tell you that not even Solomon in all his splendor was dressed like one of these. If that is how God clothes the grass of the field, which is here today and tomorrow is thrown into the fire, will he not much more clothe you, O you of little faith? So do not worry, saying, "What shall we eat?" or "What shall we drink?" or "What shall we wear?" For the pagans run after all these things, and your heavenly Father knows that you need them. But seek first his kingdom and his righteousness, and all these things will be given to you as well. Therefore do not worry about tomorrow, for tomorrow will worry about itself. Each day has enough trouble of its own.

Worry signifies doubt! Every time you put that right hand under your chin and begin to sigh in frustration, you are saying to God, "I do not trust you to see me through this." Determine today that you will live and not die. God requires one kind of death—that you die to the flesh. The number of cancer, hypertension, and diabetic cases has increased tremendously over the years. Of course, dieting plays a key role in these cases, but stress and worry have a significant impact on the victims. Believe me, when I say we serve a mighty God who specializes in making the impossibilities of humanity possible. Death is not an option for the saints because the breath of God is propelling you on.

The enemy has set out to rob the saints of joy, peace, and even prosperity, but God has given us the authority to demand the enemy to return everything he has stolen. The devil is killing our seed with drugs and HIV/AIDS, while we sit in a corner and cry. He has stolen the camaraderie of Christian leaders as we sit back embracing clerical robes and prestigious titles. Yes, the devil has destroyed our family ties as we build bigger barns and become workaholics rather than great parents. When the enemy raises its ugly head, it is not the time to panic; use the authority God has given you. As Jesus commissioned His disciples, He told them that He had all authority in heaven and in earth (Matt. 28:18). There is power in the name of Jesus Christ. You do not have to live defeated lives. When they put you in the fire or in the prison, just call on your God; He is well able to deliver you. The word of God declares in Psalm 34:19, "Many are the afflictions of the righteous: but the LORD delivereth him out of them all."

The Enemy Can Be Anyone

When the mask comes off and the truth is revealed, you will be surprised who the enemy is. The enemy is always working; he might work through your parents, children, spouse, best friend, boss, co-worker or even a stranger. In 2 Kings 11, we discovered that Athaliah attempted to destroy her very own family. "And when Athaliah the mother of Ahaziah saw that her son was dead, she arose and destroyed all the seed royal" (v. 1).

Athaliah is the daughter of Jezebel and Ahab. Athaliah worked her way from the Northern Kingdom, Israel, to the Southern Kingdom, Judah. Her desire for power and prestige made her stoop to murder. She did not succeed in her plans because God had a greater plan for that particular kingdom. Athaliah was married to Joram, or Jehoram, the son of Jehoshaphat, to whom God said the battle is not yours; it is the Lord's (2 Chron. 20:17). Joram and Athaliah had a son named Ahaziah. Yet Athaliah's heart was bent on doing evil. But in the midst of it all, a righteous seed was springing from the bowels of Jehoshaphat to the third generation.

When Ahaziah died, instead of weeping and mourning, Athaliah rejoiced. She viewed his death as an opportunity for her to rise to power, to take over his throne. Some folks eating at your table cannot wait to bury you, so they can live off your success. Ask God to give you a discerning spirit because sometimes your enemies can be those closest to you. Athaliah attempted to kill the entire royal seed, her own kindred. However, Ahaziah's sister, Jehosheba, took his son, Joash, and hid him away (2 Kings 11:2). He was a one-year-old boy who escaped the sword of his grandmother. Your spirit of discernment must be like razor because you do not know whom to trust when you are sitting in the seat of royalty.

The enemy might as well take the mask off.

Enemies camouflage themselves, pretending to be different from all the rest. They act as if they are with you, rejoicing when you are promoted. It is a front so as not to expose their true feelings. If the truth were told, they do have a problem with you. In this season you have to investigate thoroughly the persons with whom you are about to connect. You better let them identify themselves, or you might live to regret it. There is a way to know envious persons; they always want what you have. They act as if they are paying you a compliment: "Oh, that's a nice car. Where did you buy it? I love those shoes. Where did you buy them?" when in fact they are coveting. And once given the chance, they would take your very birthright. However, give your God the praise because what God has for you will never reach the tents of your enemies. Before God would give it to the enemy, He would recall the blessing. The enemy might as well take the mask off.

Let's look in more detail at 2 Kings 11:1–3 (NIV).

Athaliah and Joash

> When Athaliah the mother of Ahaziah saw that her son was dead, she proceeded to destroy the whole royal family. But Jehosheba, the daughter of King Jehoram and sister of Ahaziah, took Joash son of Ahaziah and stole him away from among the royal princes, who were about to be murdered. She put him and his nurse in a bedroom to hide him from Athaliah; so he was not killed. He remained hidden with his nurse at the temple of the LORD for six years while Athaliah ruled the land.

Joash was in the house with his brothers when Athaliah sent to have them killed. There were dead bodies all over the place! According to some theologians, the military was looking for Joash, but he was lying under a dead corpse before being taken to the bedchamber. The amazing thing is that Joash did not even cry or else they would have found him. Parents can attest to the fact that if you put a baby on the cold floor, she or he will cry. You can give that baby SMA, Gerber baby food, or oats, and that baby will still cry. I believe even an adult would scream if laid under a dead body.

Now you see why the Bible says we must become like a little child to inherit the kingdom of God. Even in danger, children display blind trust. What are you prepared to do while transitioning in the valley of dry bones? Are you screaming and pulling out your hair because of fear? Or are you prophesying to those dead bones?

As God said to Ezekiel in chapter 37, verse 4, He also says to you, "Go on and prophesy life." Take a minute and identify some areas the enemy has stolen, killed, or destroyed and begin prophesying life over them. Ah, you can do better than that; try it again. This time, use the authority given in Jesus Christ's name. I will come into agreement with you that death no longer has dominion in your finances, health, family, ministry, and so forth, in Jesus Christ's name. Amen!

Go ahead, give your God the highest praise, for you will live and not die (Ps. 118:17)! God will preserve you and the blessing, once you stay faithful to the call. Psalm 91 keeps me going when the daggers are pressing against the tendons in my back. It says in verse 5, 7–8, "Thou shalt not be afraid for the terror by night; nor for the arrow that flieth by day. . . . A thousand shall fall at thy side, and ten thousand at thy right hand; but it shall not come nigh thee. Only with thine eyes shalt thou behold and see the reward of the wicked." My God, my God, what a promise! Even in the midst of massive destruction, God is able to protect us.

Some folks are still trying to figure you out. They thought you would have been dead a long time ago. They have tried every attack possible, but you are still here. God has the final say. As I read about Athaliah's attacks, I wondered why Joash did not cry in the presence of the military as he laid among the dead corpses. How is it that a defenseless child escaped death? It is simply because God preserved him for greatness. You just need to trust God to keep you.

> *God will not let the enemy destroy you.*

You can take a fish, put salt on it, put it in the yard in the hot sun, and it would still be good when you are ready to fry it because the salt preserved it. In the same way, God preserves us when the fiery darts of our heated enemies surround us. After your mentoring circumstances, your enemies will ask, where did you come from? John the Revelator says they came through great tribulation.

God preserved Joash, and using Jehoiada the priest, He united the military and religious leaders to come up against Athaliah and slay her. The little boy Joash became king at age seven and reigned thirty-three years. God used Joash's enemy, Athaliah, to weed out everyone that would have been entitled to the throne before him and those that probably would have opposed him because Joash was His choice. God will move heaven and earth to fulfill His plans. Lord, why the enemies? To bring to pass my perfect will for your life. Come out of that cave and face the enemy; God has the last say.

God will not let the enemy destroy you; rather, the enemy will be used by God to equip you with the necessary components you will need for your maximum performance. Lord, why the enemies? To equip you for maximum performance. You may ask; "What did I do to create such animosity?" Realize that you can do all the good you can to all the people you can, as Wesleyan theology dictates, yet people will still hate you. They form collisions to destroy you because of fear of who you will become. But instead of their weapons destroying you, God will use them to build you. The attacks of your enemies are designed by God to mold you, shape you, and make you into a vessel of honor, fit for the master's use.

Your Enemies Are Designed to Usher You Into Greatness

Lord, why the enemies? To press out of you what I have placed in you. We all must pass through our Gethsemane. Gethsemane means "press or a place of pressing." I had an awesome privilege to travel to Israel in the month of June 2008, with Dr. Myles Munroe and my pastor, Apostle Leon Wallace. During this time, one of the places we visited was the Garden of Gethsemane. As I looked around in the garden, it was full of olive trees, and I wondered if it was a coincidence, that God placed olives that needed pressing to release its oil in the garden of pressing. Because we are God's olives filled with oil, He placed us in Gethsemane, or the midst of our enemies, so that they may press His anointing out of us.

The reason you are being attacked is that God is moving you to a higher place of honor. As God spoke into Jeremiah's life long ago, so He speaks to us. God says, "Before I formed thee in the belly I knew thee…and I sanctified thee" (Jer. 1:5). So, get rid of doubt and fear because God knew you before you were conceived. It is only a matter of glory. Let the enemy criticize you and call you anything else but a child of God. It does not feel so, but those persecutions are really blessings. In the Beatitudes, blessings are pronounced on the poor, mourners, and the persecuted.

> *No matter what you go through, God knows He has a child to protect.*

Moreover, Matthew 5:11–12 states, "Blessed are ye, when men revile you, and persecute you, and say all manner of evil against you falsely, for my sake. Rejoice, and be exceeding glad: for great is your reward in heaven: for so persecuted they the prophets which were before you."

God is not short on blessings; we are just too thin skinned to obtain them. The more they talk about you, the more God is going to shower down the blessings on you. No matter what you go through, God knows He has a child to protect. You might as well praise the Lord now for the victory because this fight is fixed in your favor, and the prize is greatness.

God declares you are the winner; all you need to do is show up for every fight. God has summoned your breakthrough. I agree, it is difficult to give God glory when you are broke, busted, disgusted, and your enemies are attacking from every side. However, at the end of the day, God will give you what you need to bring Him glory. If it is money to pay the bills or the anointing to destroy yokes, God has it.

God is opening doors to bring you out of the grasp of the enemy. Let them laugh! They were so sure your funeral was in sight, they called the deacon and even the bishop to help plan the service. Even if they had placed you in a wooden casket, had read the eulogy, and the undertaker started to lower the casket, God has the power to raise you from the dead. I can hear God calling, "Come forth my child." The fight is not over until God says so. All God requires is the praise.

Do not be like the woodpecker that pecked at a tree all day. Feeling exhausted, he flew away. Suddenly, the lightning flashed and the wind blew and threw the tree onto the ground. Arrogantly, the bird looked back and said, "Look what I did." It was not the woodpecker; it was God. God said when you have reached the top of the success ladder and your enemies are under your feet, look back and give the glory to the almighty Creator.

Once God has sanctified you for greatness, no one or nothing can stop you from excelling, not even your worst enemies. To be sanctified means to be set aside for delicate use. Scripturally, the sanctified is classified as light and the unsanctified as darkness. Therefore, wherever you show up, your light will outshine the darkness because light and darkness cannot be in the same room. There will always be war between light and darkness, but light will always prevail. Your enemies will cause you to shine more and more. Many will wonder what gave you such confidence, boldness, skills, and favor. Just tell them it is the Lord's doing through your enemies, and it is marvelous.

God's plan includes prosperity in every facet of your life, and no one has the power to undo what God has done. Some might say you would not last in that position. Perhaps if man had the final say; but oh, once God promotes you, no devil in hell can stand against you. God declares today that He has sanctified you; hence, you do not have to compromise your standards. There is no need to operate in timidity. Exercise your faith in the Word, and rest assured that your life is destined for greatness. Your enemies have targeted you because God has sealed you for greatness. Lord, why the enemies? To prepare you for greatness.

It is evident that the mark of God is upon you for greatness. This mark is a seal—a sign that distinguishes you from an ordinary person. Thanksgiving is one of the best times of the year to shop in America;

items are marked down half-price. These sale items are often tagged with a red dot or some other sale marker so that customers will know there is a special discount. God has also marked the saints with a peculiar label: God's anointing. God says He has set His seal, the Holy Spirit, upon us until the day of redemption. The enemy sees this mark as an invitation to test our durability and he puts up a fight. God allows the fight to bring us forth into greatness. For instance, it took Pharaoh and the Egyptians to bring Moses forth; it took Eglon and the Moabites to bring Ehud forth; it took Jabin, king of Canaan, and Sisera, the captain of his host, along with the Canaanites to bring Deborah and Barak forth; and it took the opposition of the Midianites to bring Gideon forth. Likewise, it will take some opposition to bring us forth in that place of greatness.

> *The enemy is blessing your socks off! Stop trying to get even and love them.*

Though the enemy may come in like a flood, you need to hold onto God's standards. Most Christians seem to rest their Christianity on the side, so to speak, to tangle with the enemy. Watch out how you respond to the schemes of the enemy because people are taking note of God's mark on you. They see "extraordinary" written all over you. Therefore, we cannot fight with the weaponry of the world, like Shequita and Shenanae, cursing and throwing blows. We have to fight with love, kindness, and forgiveness. This might require some fasting and extra prayers.

If Tylenol and Advil put on extra strength, so the more the children of God must put on extra strength. Jesus plainly tells us to love our enemies and pray for those that despitefully use us (Matt. 5:44). This is one of the hardest things to do: love folks who literally set out to destroy your character and love folks who try to block your promotion. How do we love our enemies? When we take God at His word. In verse 11, God said, "Blessed are ye, when men shall revile you, and persecute you, and shall say all manner of evil against you falsely, for my sake." The enemy is blessing your socks off! Stop trying to get even and love them.

Matthew 5:44 carries the key to defeating the enemy. It commands us to "Love your enemies, bless them that curse you, do good to them that hate you, and pray for them that despitefully use you, and persecute you." Wow, this is not an easy commandment to keep: love your enemy, and do good to them that hate you.

Once the enemy attacked my character so bad, I felt like literally crawling under a rock and dying. The first ounce of strength I had to kneel in prayer, I cried: Lord just wipe them off the face of the earth, kill them right now! When I was finished justifying my position, I heard the Spirit correct me: "If you love only those that love you, what reward do you have? How is this request different from that of a sinner?" I wept like a baby because the enemy had turned my loving heart into one of evil and revenge. I had to repent. When the second attack came by the hands of the same persons, my prayer language changed: I cried, Lord you are the judge, and vengeance belongs to you, so please bless my enemies as they go out and as they come in. If we are going to be victorious, we have to love unconditionally, love even those who hate us.

Artillery for the Enemies

- Be alert and vigilant. (Do not be deceived by the flattery words and false smiles.)

- Attack them with love. (Express unconditional love.)

- Confuse the enemy with kindness. (Look for opportunities to help them.)

- Be still. (Let God fight your battles.)

- Know your rights. (Stand on the authority of the word of God.)

- See your enemies as instructors. (They will equip you for greatness.)

Special Prayer for Protection From Enemies

Taken From Psalm 91

Dear Lord, You are indeed a mighty God! My enemies will not prevail against me because I am hiding in the secret place of the most High and abiding under the shadow of the Almighty. God, You are my refuge and my fortress. My God, it is in You I do trust. Surely You will deliver me from the snare of the fowler and from the noisome pestilence. You will cover me with Your feathers, and under Your wings I will trust. Your truth is my shield and buckler. I will not be afraid of the terror by night or of the arrow that flieth by day or of the pestilence that walks in darkness or of the destruction that wastes at noonday. A thousand shall fall at my side and ten thousand at my right hand, but it will not come near me. Only with my eyes, will I behold and see the reward of the wicked. I love You, Lord, and I am persuaded that You will deliver me and set me on high because I acknowledge Your name. Thank You for long life and showing me Your salvation. Amen!

Chapter 4

LORD, WHY THE REJECTION?

Rejection Makes Us Partners in Christ's Suffering

What comes to mind when you think of a king? Is it someone with authority, highly respected, powerful, wealthy, and popular? Would you have ever associated words such as rejected, despised, sorrow, dishonored, and so forth, with a king? Yet, the great prophet Isaiah gave this exact descriptive to foretell of the King of kings' reign. He decreed, "He is despised and rejected of men; a man of sorrows, and acquainted with grief: and we hid as it were our faces from him; he was despised, and we esteemed him not" (Isa. 53:3).

Most theologians assert that the reference made in this passage is to Jesus, the Messiah, Savior of the world. Surely the life of Jesus most definitely fits into Isaiah's frame of reference, for indeed, His life was fashioned by rejection from birth to the time of his death. Jesus, the King of kings, had to be born in a stable where animals were kept because there was no room in the inns. The people of his hometown refused to believe in Him because, they knew His brothers and sisters and that He was the son of the carpenter (Mark 6:3). The crowd who once shouted, "Blessed is he that cometh in the name of the Lord" (11:9), three days later cried, "Crucify him" (15:13). Lord, why the rejection?

Jesus, although the greatest being ever to have walked the face of this Earth, is the epitome of rejection. It would seem that the chore of Christianity is rooted in rejection. Webster's Dictionary defines the term rejection as "to cast off, to discard, to repel, to forsake, or to decline."[1] The Thesaurus substitutes the following nouns for rejection: "negative response, refusal, denial, rebuff, denunciation, refutation, dismissal, and elimination."[2] Rejection is hard to deal with; it makes you feel like "a nobody," as if you are not qualified or not good enough to be around a certain set of people. Often those who are rejected go into a state of depression and even sometimes become suicidal. Christians are called to rise up from the cold hands of rejection and be confident that this is all in the plan of God to bring us into our destiny. As the Bible declares in Romans 8:28, "And we know that all things work together for good to them that love God, to them who are the called according to his purpose." It was God's will for Jesus to share in the sorrow of humanity to pay the redemptive price of those estranged from God.

New Testament writers encourage Christians to rejoice when counted worthy to suffer for the sake of the Gospel. As recorded in 1 Peter 4:13–14, "But rejoice, inasmuch as ye are partakers of Christ's sufferings; that, when his glory shall be revealed, ye may be glad also with exceeding joy. If ye be reproached for the name of Christ, happy are ye; for the spirit of glory and of God resteth upon you: on their part he is evil spoken of, but on your part he is glorified."

However, how is it possible to rejoice when people befriend you with gifts and sugarcoated words while at the same time holding a knife to stab you in the back? Is it possible to be happy when you enter the room, sometimes even the house of God, and can actually feel the negative vibes, unspoken hatred, and jealousy from those present? Is it humane to give love in return for the insults, ridicule, and blatant disrespect received from family and friends? I strongly believe that when we are prepared to surrender to the will of God, we will rejoice in hardship. Jesus, our great exemplar, knew the will of God and therefore was obedient even to death. You might still be puzzled as to how or why God's will for your life would include rejection. Well, it is not until we are operating in the perfect will of God that we will be fulfilled. Lord, why the rejection? Because suffering with God qualifies you to reign with God.

Rejection Aligns Us With the Will of God

There is a place in God that allows us to operate in His perfect will. The adversary would do anything in his power to stop us from attaining this because he knows of the joy and security that is there. Stop letting the rejection of people discourage you from achieving your goals, and be confident that God's plan is set, established, and in place for your life. Do you realize that God has already calculated every move you make? God has predestinated, predetermined, and foreordained such a place for us. It is a place where we walk in the fullness of faith, one hundred fold anointing, health and strength, authority, provision, peace, and joy. It is in this place that we have access to abundance, for we have matured to a level where we can receive the overflow and remain faithful to the great Provider. Whatever we encounter as Christians, God is aware, and He is allowing it so that His will might be fulfilled in our lives.

> *Let go, and let God direct the traffic.*

God is leading us to opportunities that will lead to success. Let go, and let God direct the traffic. Some folks would have you believe in coincidence, luck, or happenstance. I maintain that nothing happens by chance; there is no such thing as luck in the life of a chosen vessel of God. Everything that we encounter, whether great or small, is significant to our maturing in God.

The story is told of a man who wanted life insurance. In the interview, the agent asked him if he had ever been in an accident. He replied no. Then after a while, he admitted that he was once bitten by a rattlesnake and kicked by a horse. The agent was confused and said, "But you just told me you where never in an accident!" He said, "Yes, I told you I was never in an accident because it was not an accident. The snake meant to bite me, and the horse meant to kick me." Some folks were ordained to shut the door in our faces so that we could pick up our things and head toward the pathway of God. Lord, why the rejection? To align us with God's will and purpose for our lives.

As humans, we are prone to wander out of the will of God and to embrace our selfish desires. It is often in these times that God allows us to be cast off to bring us back in line with His will. Yes, even the most respected Christians rebel against God's mandate. I am sure you know the story of Jonah, a prophet of God, who, after being thrown into the angry ocean, spent three days in the belly of a whale. Jonah decided to disobey God's perfect will: God wanted Jonah in Nineveh, but he opted to take a boat to Tarshish (Jon. 1:1–3).

God will disrupt the plans of men to achieve His perfect will, even if He has to conspire with nature. Disobedience can lead to serious consequences; the boat was almost capsized, and the lives of those men were uncertain. Rejection came to Jonah as the men threw him overboard (v. 15). It was the only way to get Jonah into Nineveh and to save their lives. You see, when we refuse to obey God, we put persons around us in jeopardy as well. We must remember that God's directive is to bring life. Like Jonah, we might be inclined to resist, fearing that God would be merciful and our message rendered null and void. However, when God speaks, it is our duty to obey and not try to predetermine God's moves.

Remember, nothing can happen to you except what God allows; and it will occur only for your good. If God permits us to be treated nice and loved in the environment we are in and around the people we so desire to accompany, we will remain average. Some people in your life might be mistreating you; maybe this is because God is trying to redirect you to follow His perfect will. Joseph said to his brothers who had abandoned him in a pit then sold him into slavery, "But as for you, ye thought evil against me; but God meant it unto good, to bring to pass, as it is this day, to save much people alive" (Gen. 50:20).

When people who used to love you suddenly cannot stand your guts, God says, "I am fully aware and it's only a process." It is only a matter of time before God flips the script so that you can see the good in all that pain. The word of God declares in Isaiah 40:31, "But they that wait upon the LORD shall renew their strength; they shall mount up with wings as eagles; they shall run, and not be weary; and they shall walk, and not faint." You need not get weary or slack your ride; God will lift up a standard so that those who once scorned you will bow in reverence to you. Lord, why the rejection? To take you beyond the status quo of your present environment!

Rejection Is Direction

Too often Christians become comfortable in certain environments, thus remaining stagnated. Regardless of the lack of growth, we tend to desire these surroundings because they are familiar. Often God has to

> *Before we die, God is snatching us up and throwing us into our rightful place.*

allow a crisis to unfold to move us away from such places. If we were to be honest with ourselves for a second, we would have to agree that we have resided in such places and might still be in them today if God did not let the gatekeepers reject us. Those discarders are going to move us into the environment that will cause us to grow, expand, and flourish in the kingdom of God.

In nature, every living thing has its prescribed environment. For example, the fish's environment is the sea, the bird's environment is the sky, and our environment is the presence of God; that is where you find His perfect will. A fish is at its best when it is in the water; it swims, breathes, and thrives with ease. However, take the fish out of the water and place it on land and it becomes helpless and eventually dies. I was at Potter's Cay Dock in Nassau one day and the fishing boats were all lined across the harbor. I stopped to greet a friend. I could not help but notice a fish wiggling its body frantically on the deck of the boat. It wiggled itself to death. I also noticed the fishermen sorting through their catch. They threw the baby fish back into the sea. As the fish landed in the water, they began to flap their fins and swam away. God has ordained us to be in a certain place, and most of us are so caught up with the cares of this life that we have been transported to other territories. Before we die, God is snatching us up and throwing us into our rightful place. Lord, why the rejection? It is for direction.

Let's look at the story of the four lepers as written in 2 Kings 7 for a clearer understanding of how rejection can direct us into the will of God.

The Siege Lifted

Elisha said, "Hear the word of the Lord. This is what the Lord says: About this time tomorrow, a seah of flour will sell for a shekel and two seahs of barley for a shekel at the gate of Samaria." The officer on whose arm the king was leaning said to the man of God, "Look, even if the Lord should open the floodgates of the heavens, could this happen?" "You will see it with your own eyes," answered Elisha, "but you will not eat any of it!" Now there were four men with leprosy at the entrance of the city gate. They said to each other, "Why stay here until we die? If we say, 'We'll go into the city'—the famine is there, and we will die. And if we stay here, we will die. So let's go over to the camp of the Arameans and surrender. If they spare us, we live; if they kill us, then we die." At dusk they got up and went to the camp of the Arameans. When they reached the edge of the camp, not a man was there, for the Lord had caused the Arameans to hear the sound of chariots and horses and a great army, so that they said to one another, "Look, the king of Israel has hired the Hittite and Egyptian kings to attack us!" So they got up and fled in the dusk and abandoned their tents and their horses and donkeys. They left the camp as it was and ran for their lives. The men who had leprosy reached the edge of the camp and entered one of the tents. They ate and drank, and carried away silver, gold and clothes, and went off and hid them. They returned and entered another tent and took some things from it and hid them also. Then they said to each other,

"We're not doing right. This is a day of good news and we are keeping it to ourselves. If we wait until daylight, punishment will overtake us. Let's go at once and report this to the royal palace." So they went and called out to the city gatekeepers and told them, "We went into the Aramean camp and not a man was there—not a sound of anyone—only tethered horses and donkeys, and the tents left just as they were." The gatekeepers shouted the news, and it was reported within the palace.

—2 Kings 7:1-11, NIV

The book of 2 Kings gives the history of the Northern Kingdom, Israel with the capital in Samaria, and the Southern Kingdom Judea, the capital being Jerusalem. The ruling king of Israel at the time was Jehoram, the prophet was Elisha, successor to Elijah, and commerce was the order of the day. The city of Samaria was a place where much trading took place; it was blessed with the finest jewelry, gold, diamonds, and other precious stones. Due to the economic success and great prosperity, the Israelites became arrogant and self-centered. They only associated with a select group of people and were known to disassociate with others.

Some folks were actually pushed out or denied access to the city. What will you do when they push you out?

The Israelites were witnesses to the awesomeness of God's ability to make a way where it seemed like there was no way. They were fortunate to experience His handiworks in the wilderness when He made the sky to rain down manna and quail for them to eat. However, the Israelites forgot that God brought them success. They rebelled against the great Provider, exchanging reverence to the Creator for worship to that which was created. Moreover, Israel disobeyed God's commandment by mingling with the neighboring nations and adopting their immoral practices. God was displeased with Israel and allowed famine to overtake the land. Hence, those who once enjoyed the delicacies of life were now struggling to find a morsel of bread. The people were desperate enough to consume human babies and dove's dung as food! Nevertheless, the famine was merely a temporary disposition, designed to bring Israel back to humility and awe of God.

As we discovered in the scripture, those who were cast out of the city, the four lepers, became the Israelite heroes. The prophet had brought a word that the people could not imagine to be true because of their present condition. Elisha had prophesied that before the day was over, the same scarce commodities would be available in abundance. Yet they were so occupied with their present situation that they could not even receive the word of God. One of the king's noblemen, whom he depended on for counsel, answered the man of God and said, "Even if God opened the windows of heaven, how could this be?" (v. 2). They had not developed enough faith in God to believe He could miraculously shift the supply and demand curve so that the once economic deficit could be annulled. In the space of a day, their situation was changed. God has a way of using the rejects of the world to bring about great exploits.

At that time of their expulsion from the city, I could imagine the grief these lepers were feeling, having to leave behind family and friends and their personal belongings. Probably they felt this was the end of their lives. According to many theologians, lepers were not allowed inside the cities or among people. When passersby approached the town that they were dwelling near, the lepers were to shout "unclean, unclean" to warn them not to come in the vicinity. This was a law established by God under the Mosaic covenant.

Leprosy is described as a progressive infectious disease of the skin, flesh, and nerves, characterized by ulcers, white scaly scabs, and deformation. The priest normally diagnosed the sickness and set the prescribed remedy. Depending on the diagnosis, homes had to be burnt down and utensils sanitized.

God told Moses in Leviticus that all the days that the leprosy is found in them, they should be put out of the camp (13:46).

The same God who established the law that worked against the lepers is a law within Himself. The revised law was a command to the lepers to get up and go toward the enemy's camp.

A person with leprosy suffered both socially, emotionally, and financially. This was not a good state in which to be! Lord, why the rejection?

> *We must trust God's leadership because He has the big picture in front of Him.*

These four rejected, unwanted lepers were so desperate to get into the city that they kept watch at the gate. There are times when what looks like prosperity and the better life is just a façade. So often people run from one church to the other or from job to job. Some even exchange spouses as they change clothing, hoping to receive better. You might recall the old adage, "the grass always looks greener on the other side." So it seemed initially in the case of the lepers. That is, the state of the city looked more fertile than outside the gate, but this was not the case. Little did they know that God had a purpose as He assented to their being infected with leprosy and thus thrown out of the city. Had these four men stayed in the city, their faith would not have stood the test.

We must trust God's leadership because He has the *big* picture in front of Him. A father brought his son a 500-piece puzzle. The son struggled for a long time trying to figure out how to put the puzzle together, staring at two pieces he held in his hands. His dad observed as the boy became more frustrated at each failed attempt. Finally the father mercifully exclaimed, "Give it to me." Within half an hour he completed the puzzle. With amazement the son asked his father, "How is it that you were so quick to solve the puzzle?" The father responded, "You were merely looking at the two pieces, while I was looking at the whole picture." It is so easy to substitute the character of Jesus for the father in this story, and we fit the description of the son.

In our failure, all we see are the broken pieces, the hard places, and rejection. The apostle Paul tells us that we see through a glass dimly (1 Cor. 13:12), but oh, I am so glad that God has 20/20 vision and clearly sees the end of a matter. Lord, why the rejection? To sharpen our insight and vision for the journey ahead!

The Rejected Stone Is the Cornerstone

If only we could see into the future, just maybe our response to others would be different. One thing is certain, regardless of how successful we become, there will come a time when we will all need someone else. John Donne, an English poet, wrote a serious of meditations and prayers while recovering from a serious illness. A line from Meditation XVII insisted that human beings do not thrive isolated from each other: "No man is an island, entire of itself; every man is a piece of the continent, a part of the main."[3]

A good friend of mine, Nora, shared her story about the broken relationship she had with her father. Her father blatantly refused to own her as his daughter. The rejection of a parent really hurts! Many children are acting out by joining gangs or getting pregnant as teens because of such rejection. Nora cried many times, longing for her father's embrace, but he openly refused. Eventually he became very ill, at the point of death, and she received a phone call to visit him. She found him lying on a bed at Princess Margaret Hospital in The Bahamas. He was hungry and asked for soup. She purchased the soup and fed him as if he were a baby. Despite all of this, he still refused to acknowledge her as his child. She still rejoiced, concluding that God had given her, the rejected stone, an opportunity to be a cornerstone.

God has a way of using the rejects of the world to bring about great exploits. In a similar vein, God used these four lepers to reap the harvest of the land. One would think the Israelite army or governing body would be the ones to bring relief rather than these men. God messed up my theology: why would He let four defenseless lepers head towards the Syrian army, a group of renegades who were armed and dangerous? However, in 2 Kings 7:5–6, it reads:

> And they rose up in the twilight, to go unto the camp of the Syrians: and when they were come to the uttermost part of the camp of Syria, behold, there was no man there. For the LORD had made the host of the Syrians to hear a noise of chariots, and

a noise of horses, even the noise of a great host: and they said one
to another, Lo, the king of Israel hath hired against us the kings
of the Hittites, and the kings of the Egyptians, to come upon us.

They had finally tagged in Jesus, Jehovah Sabbaoth, the Lord of
hosts. God went before the lepers and caused the enemy to flee; leaving
the spoils that was predestined and predetermined for the four lepers'
to inherit. You might as well dry those tears because God has a plan, no
matter how they reject you, spit on you, or deny you access. God will
use the vessel of His choosing to bring deliverance. God has chosen you
to excel despite the rejection.

God chose the four lepers to inherit the enemies' spoils, these same
outcast men as the vehicle of wealth into Samaria. We need to be careful
how we look down on others. You may be surprised to know who is a
carrier of God's blessing. The adverse condition faced by the city was
about to change by four unwanted, despised lepers. These men had
faith coupled with their works, and that was all they needed to succeed.
I heard God say, "If you ask me I will make a way out of no way." Stay
on that job, in your church, with your spouse; God has destined you to
bring about change. Solomon was on to something when he observed
that the race is not given to the swiftest or strongest (Eccles. 9:11). It
is given to the one who endures. This is no time to give up. The lepers
waited patiently, and one day, God made them shine among those that
once scorned them.

The city is not where the victory lies, so you have to take your eyes
off the city. The blessing is on the outskirts of town. Do not cry when
people reject you; it is a prescribed plan by the master Himself. There
may be a Jaguar in the yard of the
neighbor who is living like the devil,
they may be going on cruises, and the
power company may never shut off
their electricity; however, you on the
other hand are suffering, going through

> *There is a set time
> in God, and we have
> to endure until that
> time is fully come*

all kinds of struggles. You do not seem to understand why the heathens are so popular, and you are not.

Those lepers must have also been confused. Maybe if it was some of us, we might not return to the house of God. Yet, God has a way to make us stay where we do not want to be. If it takes rejection to get you to your destiny, you will get there.

When you truly trust God, you will stop looking at other people's anointing, power and gifts. Can you imagine the lepers sitting there watching them in the city eating and drinking extravagantly and enjoying the overflow, while they struggled to find a crumb of bread. Many are experiencing these same conditions daily as the lepers did; for instance, while others are getting a raise, promotion, and living it up on the perks, you have to stay in your corner, barely making ends meet. Just remember, God has a plan.

There is a set time in God, and we have to endure until that time is fully come. It is useless to look to those who are arrayed in fancy attire, educated in worldly affairs, or eloquent in speech. God is using the humble—those unpopular and insignificant Christians—to usher in the harvest. Lord, why the rejection? God wants people who are pure in heart and dedicated to Him to express His glory upon the Earth. Grab your spiritual rope and hold on. So what are you going to do: weep and complain or do great exploits?

This generation, often referred to as Generation X, who by the world's standard is destined to fail. In this generation are those whom God, however, has predestined to do great exploits in the name of Jesus Christ. Exploits in this case means "what has never been heard of in spiritual history." Lord, why the rejection? To move you from the familiar to the unfamiliar, positioning you for greatness.

Rejection provides stamina to go unknowingly into a gold mine

With a little more faith, you will be in that number; all you have to do is step out of the boat. So many people dream of obtaining riches, becoming anointed, and winning the lost at any cost, but these things require more than mere lip service; you need to back it up with action. James says, "Faith without works is dead" (2:20). It took faith for the lepers to take their eyes off Samaria and to go into the enemy's camp. We have to make up in our minds to go wherever God leads, even if it means running through troops and leaping over walls. The devil will have to move out of the way when he sees you coming for your possession.

Rejection provides stamina to go unknowingly into a gold mine. When people around me pronounced doom and failure upon my goals, my initial response was, "Lord, why me?" Then I shook myself, as if it were merely a bad dream, and doubled my efforts to achieve my goals. Rejection is a tough blow, but you have been built with all it takes to survive it. The first tent the lepers entered had more than enough supplies, including gold and silver; they hid them. Moving into the second tent, they did the same. Eventually, they decided to let the others know of their discovery. It is tempting to hide our blessings from those that rejected us, but in obedience, we must do what God requires of us: to bless them that curse us. What joy must have engulfed these lepers as they took the spoils!

Think of something you have been struggling with and then start to rejoice, assured that God is reversing the situation. Long ago, my friends and I meaninglessly sang the words to the song "I Can See Clearly Now." When you take God at His word, you, too, can sing with assurance, "It's going to be a bright sunshiny day." Someone once said God is like Maxwell House—good to the last drop. He is like scotch tape—you cannot see Him, but He holds your life together. He is like American Express—don't leave home without Him, or like VO5 hair spray—holds up in any kind of weather. He is like your power company—He will light up your life. Stay in God, for your life is about to be renewed. This is your season; your change is on the way. Isaiah declared, "But they that wait upon the LORD shall renew their strength; they shall mount up with wings as eagles; they shall run, and not be weary; and they shall walk, and not faint" (Isa: 40:31). Go ahead, go on and sing with joy, for those days of discouragement and illness are gone away. God is shining on your condition.

Rejection Is Not Final

Think it not strange concerning the fiery trials, for they are designed to bring out the power and anointing that God has placed in you. We can learn a lesson to this effect from the science of bodybuilding. Every time a person lifts weights, it brings out bigger and stronger muscles. According to Richard Mitchell, "In order for muscle to grow, three things are required:

1. *Stimulus*—exercise is needed to make the muscles work, use energy, and cause microscopic damage to the fibers.

2. *Nutrition*—after intense exercise, the muscles need to replenish their stores of fuel.

3. *Rest*—it is during the rest or recovery that the muscles repair the microscopic damage and grow."[4]

So it is with the trials of life, with rejection being one of the worst to encounter; it strengthens, stretches, and matures us. So, let them throw weight on us; it is going to give us bigger, stronger, and more supple spiritual muscles. Recall the last crisis that you encountered; I bet while going through the experience, you felt it would kill you. When you look back at that occurrence, don't you feel a little stronger as a result? Hasn't your faith in God's ability to keep you in adverse times increased?

Moreover, because of our hardship, we gain a testimony, a story to share with others who are going through their crisis. Someone once said that without a test, we could not have a testimony. To take this cliché a little further, I would venture to say that without problems, we would never know that God could solve them. Oh, how drastic our response to the challenges of life will change when we realize that we have nothing to lose by trusting God.

In 2 Kings 7:4, the lepers realized if they went in the city, they would die because the famine was in the city. If they stayed at the gate, they would still die. However, if they went in the direction of the enemy, the Syrians, they might die. In order to get what God has for you, you must get up, regroup, turn back, and fight with tools of persistence and courage. Lord, why the rejection? Well, whenever your intention is to walk out on the will of God, He allows you to become infected with problems, adverse situations, and circumstances as a means of redirecting you back to Him and His perfect will.

Do you feel overly burdened and confused because of rejection? It is a difficult pill to swallow, but in the midst of this terrible experience, know that God has a plan. You might be saying it is clear that people do not want you in the city; well, just stay out. God's hand is not so short that He cannot reach you out there.

One of the biggest problems among Christians is that we spend needless time trying to prove ourselves to people. We use all of our energy trying to measure up to their standards and fit into their world. God made us unique; we cannot discard God's handiwork to fit the mold of men. They may reject you because of your color, looks, dress style, family background, or socio-economic standards. Just remember that what others think does not matter. God has the final say, and He knows just how to esteem us among those who cast us aside as hopeless.

The lepers concluded that whether they ventured in the city or stayed out by the gate, death was eminent. However, there was a slim chance of surviving in the enemy's camp. What a tough decision to make! How do you respond when death is closing in on you? Do you evaluate every possibility for life, or do you lie down and wait for death? The lepers took a chance by going into the enemy's camp. Having nothing to lose, they sensed a possibility to survive there.

God steps in the midst of our hopelessness to bring life! The lepers were prepared to enter the enemy's camp at any cost. Here is the revelation I found in this passage: The Israelites were not the lepers' enemies because they did not have the promise. The city looked like the promise, but it was not. The Syrians were their real enemies. They had possession of the promise that belonged to the four lepers. God only used the Israelites to push them in the right direction.

Medical research indicates that leprosy may also cause deformity. Some of us are existing with deformed lives. The enemy has messed us up to the point that everything around us is deformed, our marriage and family life are deformed, and even the church is experiencing deformity. However, times of rejection destroy pride, remove false security in our own abilities, and reinforce dependency on God, which in turn will bring right formation to our lives. There are times when God allows preachers to come to the pulpit dumbfounded so they can grab onto God for a "word." May we realize it is not by might nor by power, but by the Spirit of the Lord that we are ambassadors of Jesus Christ (Zech. 4:6).

> *God steps in the midst of our hopelessness to bring life!*

God has a way to confound the enemy. By the time God is finished shaping us, our enemies will not see our flaws, but merely perfection in God. The lepers remarked, "Why sit we here until we die?" (2 Kings 7:3). This remark of the lepers reminds me of the scripture that tells us that unless a grain of wheat falls to the ground and dies, it will not spring up (John 12:24). Dying brings life: the only way to experience resurrection power is to die.

God causes stuff we are leaning on to die—relationships, help, and so forth—not to destroy us, but to change our sense of direction. Have you ever desired a car, gone to the dealers, test driven the car, and slipped away to the bank for the deposit? When you return, the car is gone, sold. This same car had been sitting on the car lot for months, but as soon as you set your eyes on it, someone else shows up to purchase it. God quickly placed in someone else's spirit to buy it because that was not what He had in mind for you. Lord, why the rejection? God has a better deal in mind for you.

This season of rejection is a temporary disposition. I believe the frustration experienced during the delay is often confused with denial. To deny is to refuse to grant a request, to not receive it, or to change one's mind. Delay, on the other hand, is a temporary disposition. God is a God of order; He does everything at the time appointed. In the natural you would not show up for a three o'clock appointment at one o'clock and expect to be attended to before those who were scheduled at that time. Nor could you have such unrealistic expectations in the spiritual. We must never confuse being delayed with being denied.

Those of you who travel on commercial airlines are acquainted with waiting for delayed flights. You sit in the departure area watching people who arrived after you, leave before you, while you sip on tea. Hence, you have to wait for the Agent to call your flight. Once you are actually sitting on the plane, the flight still does not take off until it receives clearance to fly from the tower. Remember, that God is in control and when the time comes, He will clear you for takeoff. He is at work fixing stuff in our lives so that when we take off, onlookers will be amazed of how high we soar; for we will boldly go where no man has ever gone before. Lord, why the rejection? To take you where no man has ever gone before!

Medicine for Rejection

- Develop a personal relationship with Jesus Christ. (He will send you the Comforter.)

- Stop wasting your energy on those who have left. (Celebrate your supporters.)

- Be an optimist. (See it as a stepping stone into the future.)

- Learn from each experience. (It is a way of maturing.)

- Praise that heavy spirit off. (God is moved by our praise.)

- This is all in the plan. (Remind yourself daily that God has a plan to prosper you.)

Special Prayers for the Rejected

Taken from 1 Peter 4:12–13

Dear God, I pray that I do not think it strange concerning the fiery trial that is to try me, as though some strange thing happened to me, but that I will rejoice to the extent that I partake of Christ's sufferings, so that when His glory is revealed, I may also be glad with exceeding joy. Amen!

Chapter 5

LORD, NOW I KNOW WHY!

The frustration of the wilderness, jealousy, enemies, and rejection often hides the truth of God's active presence. Frequently the initial response is to crawl into a corner, blanketing our fears with feelings of abandonment and confusion. Lord, why? Why the wilderness, jealousy, enemies, and rejection? The answer to this tone of questioning is given in increments and probably never fully understood until the end of the trial. However, we can be assured that these experiences are designed to usher us into the promises of God. This might be difficult to grasp, especially if you are in the midst of a "fiery furnace" at this very moment. Yet, as King Solomon, known in Christendom as the wisest king to have ever reigned, declared, "Man's goings are of the Lord; how can a man then understand his own way?" (Prov. 20:24). If your goings and my goings are of the Lord, we must realize that God will always direct us according to His divine will. Hence, it is in our best interest to follow God's direction.

It is so easy to go off track when wondering through the terrain of repudiation, resentment, and adversity. Nevertheless, the encounter of opposition from so

> *Once we have survived the school of hard knocks, we are ready to pour into the lives of the hopeless, downtrodden, and the oppressed.*

called supporters, the snares set by covetous colleagues, and the confrontation of the foe will sharpen our discernment and strengthen our endurance capacity. The apostle Paul explained it best when he exclaimed, "Now I say that the heir, as long as he is a child, differeth nothing from a servant, though he be lord of all; But is under tutors and governors until the time appointed of the father" (Gal. 4:1–2). Here Paul infers that as long as the "heir" is inexperienced, immature, or still a child, he is in no better position than a servant of his father, although everything belongs to him. In order for him to receive the promise of the father at the appointed time, he must be placed under tutors and governors. You might be prone to ask why. Well, what disqualified the heir, and us, from receiving the promise is subsequently changed by tutoring—the wilderness, jealousy, enemies, and rejection.

Yes, my friends, God allows us to go through a series of training just like a soldier before given a weapon, a pilot before flying a plane, or a surgeon before operating on a patient. So the heirs of the promises of God must be fully trained, equipped, and matured for the task ahead. Once we have survived the school of hard knocks, we are ready to pour into the lives of the hopeless, downtrodden, and the oppressed. All that we need to associate with men of high esteem and noblemen is realized through such training.

> *All these experiences are just teachers, trainers, educators, and instructors.*

The stretching and maturing that occurs during adversity puts pep in our step that the jealous rivals cannot duplicate. Do you recall when Moses stood before Pharaoh? Pharaoh's magicians and sorcerers were only allowed to imitate Moses in performing some of the signs. (See Exodus 7.) However, when God wanted to make the distinction, they were not able to copy certain plagues. God has taken you through the dangerous courts of the Pharaoh; be vigilant and stay the course because in the end, you will only see the remains of the enemies floating on the bed of a dead sea.

The experience of the wilderness, jealousy, enemies, and rejection are God's teachers, trainers, educators, and instructors which are designed to bring us to a place of maturity and perfection. This will then bring about the release of the greater—greater anointing, greater power, greater favor, greater wealth, and greater everything. A few weeks ago, I tried to comfort a Christian colleague with these exact sentiments. Overwhelmed with grief and the cares of this life, he responded hysterically, "Are you out of your mind? How can this continuous feeling of loneliness, along with those jealous and envious people attacking me for what rightly belongs to me, coupled with the sleepless nights, not mentioning the enemies on every side trying their best to destroy me with vicious, cunning plots, or when those that I called family and friends, my leaning post, my confidante, suddenly reject me, leaving me vulnerable to the cold, heat, and the haters result in a greater anointing?" I invited him, as I now invite you, to meditate on Romans 8:28, which states, "And we know that all things work together for good to them that love God, to them who are the called according to his purpose." All these experiences are just teachers, trainers, educators, and instructors.

"But God, why? Isn't there another way to get us to our destiny?" you might ask. Well, the experience of the wilderness, jealousy, enemies, and rejection will actually give us the practical skills necessary to fulfill our purpose. The psalmist exclaims, "My soul shall make her boast in the LORD: the humble shall hear thereof, and be glad" (Ps. 34:2). The further the enemy pushes us into pits of despair, the more doors will fling open for us to boast in the Lord. Friends, God never intended for us to look at the muck and grim that lies at the bottom of the pit; God desires we look to the hills from whence cometh our help (121:1).

I have proven that when I take my eyes off the situation and look at the Master who defines Himself as the great I Am, I begin to see things differently. I had many struggles, but in the midst of them, I was able to boast in the Lord. During financial crisis, God revealed Himself as Jehovah Jireh, my Provider. When sickness attacked, God stepped on the scene as Jehovah Rophe, my Healer. Once my enemies tried all they could to frustrate me, my God showed up as Jehovah Shalom, my

Prince of Peace. Hallelujah, praise the Lord; I endured the test because now I have a testimony!

A confident student is not easily distracted; moreover, a student who has studied and done the necessary preparation for an exam is confident during the test. (I must confess that during the initial attacks, I lacked confidence; but as I matured in God, I stood my ground.) Your testing is only for a season, and then you, too, will be assured of the power that lies within you.

Have you ever observed a baby learning to walk? My oldest daughter, Ranae', was always clever. As a baby, she was determined to walk without the aid of an adult. One day as I held out my hand beckoning her to walk to me, Ranae' tried with all her might to stand up firmly. She successfully made two steps and fell to the ground. This went on for quite some time, and every time she fell, she screamed, not so much from the fall, but out of fear and frustration. Eventually Ranae' made four steps, then ten, and so on. Now she is walking, running, and jumping with confidence. Endure your testing as a good soldier because at the end of the day you will be leaping for joy.

> *A confident student is not easily distracted; moreover, a student who has studied and done the necessary preparation for an exam is confident during the test.*

The lyrics sung by Tye Tribbett in the song "Still Have Joy" are ringing in my ears. Tye sings about still having joy after many trials. How often our joy is sapped away by the experiences of the wilderness, jealousy, enemies, and rejection. Tribbett seemed to suggest in this song that it is possible to have joy when the smoke of trials and tribulation fades away. Tribbett alludes to what the psalmist admonishes in Psalm 30:50, "Weeping may endure for a night, but joy comes in the morning."

I want to let you know that the easiest way to confuse your enemies is to rejoice when they throw those fiery darts at you. The enemy expects you to get angry, crawl up in a hole, and wait to die. However, if you dare to hum one of those sweet hymns and greet your opponents with the biggest smile ever, even though they are against you and plotting to destroy you, it will leave them speechless. Your weapon is love when attacked with hatred, kindness when knocked down by envy, and joy when all hell breaks loose.

In conclusion, I want to re-emphasize that your mentoring circumstances designed by God—wilderness, jealousy, enemies, and rejection—will work out for your good. Remember, God commanded in the Gospel of Matthew chapter 5 and verse 44, "But I say unto you, Love your enemies, bless them that curse you, do good to them that hate you, and pray for them which despitefully use you, and persecute you." Once we keep this statute, God will fight our battles.

You might be asking, "What's taking God so long to enter the fight?" The reason God is so relaxed is that He has written the script, and He knows what the end is going to be. God knows that no matter how the wilderness, jealousy, enemies, or rejection comes, in the end, you are going to be the victor. God told Jeremiah in chapter 29:11, "For I know the thoughts that I think towards you, saith the Lord, thoughts of peace, and not of evil, to give you an expected end." God has great plans for our lives and He has already put everything in motion for them to be realized. We, being the apex of God's creation and His representatives here on Earth, must conclude in our mind and spirit that if God allows us to experience the wilderness, jealousy, enemies, and rejection, He has a divine purpose for it.

Special Prayer to Understand the Will of God

Taken From 2 Corinthians 4:8–9

Dear Lord, I pray that I remember that, though I am hard-pressed on every side, I am not crushed; I am perplexed, but not in despair; persecuted, but not forsaken; struck down, but not destroyed. Amen.

About the Author

Apostle Dr. Reno I. Johnson is a man guided by the Holy Spirit; he is an ambassador of Christ, he is a Warrior in the faith, an excellent Teacher of God's Word and a Dynamic, Radical Preacher. In addition, he is an author, who has written many books that have broaden the scope of individuals globally and they have helped to usher lost souls into the Kingdom of God. In every dispensation throughout biblical history God has chosen men after his own heart. There was Moses, Joshua, David, Elijah, Paul, and now in our generation Apostle Johnson. He is the son of Patricia and Ivan Johnson. He is married to Shandaly Johnson and has one son and two daughters.

Apostle Johnson was ordained as a Minister at The Voice of Deliverance Disciple Center Ministries, Nassau Bahamas where he served for over thirteen years. By divine appointment today, the call and power of God is being demonstrated in the life of Apostle Johnson in such an awesome way. His unconditional love for people and passion for God's Word has been a transportation that has taken him throughout The World at large preaching the Good News of the Gospel of Jesus Christ.

Most notably, he is the president and Chief Executive Officer (CEO) of Reno I. Johnson Ministries International. He was consecrated to the Office of an Apostle on Sunday, December 5, 2010. He is also the founding pastor of Total Life Church, Altamonte Springs, Florida and Divine Encounter Ministries International in Nassau, The Bahamas.

Equally important, he has obtained an Associate Degree from New England Institute of Technology- West Palm Beach, Florida. However, upon receiving the call to ministry Apostle Johnson pursued several Biblical Degrees including a Diploma in Biblical Studies from Liberty University (Lynchburg, Virginia), an Associate Degree in Biblical Studies, and also an Honorary Doctorate Degree in Theology from Bethel Christian University, At present, he is pursuing higher academia in Theology.

Apostle Johnson is a highly sought after anointed messenger of God, whose passion is to win souls for Christ, and advance the Kingdom of God. "**Touching people, Transforming lives**"

CONTACT THE AUTHOR

You can email the author at
rijmintl@gmail.com or renoijohnson@gmail.com

Please visit the author's website for current phone numbers
and address.
www.arjm.org

To order any of Apostle Dr. Reno I. Johnson's Ministry Resources
Please visit our website, write or call us Today!

For Speaking Engagements please call, email or visit our website Today.

Connect with us on social media

Don't forget to visit our Website!

NOTES

Introduction

1. Webster's New World Dictionary and Thesaurus (Springfield MA: Merriam-Webster, 2002), s.v. "Wilderness."

2. The American Heritage Dictionary, s.v. "Wilderness."

Chapter 1
Lord, Why the Wilderness?

1. Carl Jung quote from 1934, http://www.netposterworks.com/quotes/jungquote.html (accessed September 14, 2009).

2. Webster's Dictionary and Thesaurus, s.v. "Desensitize."

Chapter 2
Lord, Why the Jealousy?

1. Berlitz Dictionary of American English, s.v. "Jealousy."

2. Ibid, s.v. "Envy or Envious."

3. Wikipedia article "Jealousy," http://en.wikipedia.org/wiki/Jealousy (accessed September 15, 2009).

4. William Shakespeare, Othello, act 3, scene 3.

Chapter 3
Lord, Why the Enemies?

1. Navy UDT-SEAL Museum, "BUD/S" article, http://www.navy-sealmuseum.com/heritage/training_buds.php (accessed September 16, 2009).

2. Patriot Missile Air Defense System, USA, http://www.army-technology.com/projects/patriot/ (accessed September 16, 2009).

Chapter 4
Lord, Why the Rejection?

1. Webster's Dictionary and Thesaurus, s.v. "Rejection."

2. Webster's Dictionary and Thesaurus, s.v. "Rejection."

3. John Donne, Devotions upon Emergent Occasions, no. 17, originally published in 1624, http://quotationsbook.com/quote/44607/ (accessed September 17, 2009).

4. Richard Mitchell, "What Causes Muscle Growth," http://www.specialtyansweringservice.net/articles/build-muscle/What-Causes-Muscle-Growth_6523/ (accessed September 17, 2009).

Other Books By The Author

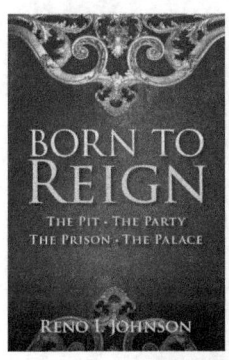 

CPSIA information can be obtained
at www.ICGtesting.com
Printed in the USA
LVHW032015180820
663535LV00021B/668